A-Z CHE

CW00541654

CONTENTS

Key to Map Pages	2-3
Map Pages	4-43
Large Scale Map Page	44
Index to Villages, ...nd selected Places of Interest	45-60

REFERENCE

Motorway	**M53**	Car Park (selected)	**P**
A Road	**A55**	Church or Chapel	†
B Road	**B5129**	Cycleway (selected)	
Dual Carriageway		Fire Station	■
One Way Street — Traffic flow on A Roads is indicated by a heavy line on the driver's left.		Hospital	**H**
		House Numbers (A & B Roads only)	13 8
Restricted Access		Information Centre	**i**
Pedestrianized Road		National Grid Reference	²85
Track / Footpath		Park & Ride	Wrexham Road **P+**
Residential Walkway		Police Station	▲
Railway — Level Crossing / Station / Tunnel		Post Office	★
		Toilet: without facilities for the Disabled	▽
		with facilities for the Disabled	▽
Built Up Area		Viewpoint	
City Wall		Educational Establishment	
National Boundary	+·+·+·+	Hospital or Hospice	
Local Authority Boundary	—·—·—	Industrial Building	
Posttown Boundary		Leisure or Recreational Facility	
Postcode Boundary within Posttown	— — —	Place of Interest	
Map Continuation	**15** Large Scale City Centre **44**	Public Building	
		Shopping Centre or Market	
		Other Selected Buildings	

SCALE

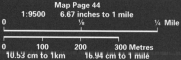

Map Pages 4-43
1:19000 3.33 inches to 1 mile
0   ¼   ½ Mile
0   250   500   750 Metres
5.26cm to 1km   8.47cm to 1 mile

Map Page 44
1:9500 6.67 inches to 1 mile
0   ⅛   ¼ Mile
0   100   200   300 Metres
10.53 cm to 1km   16.94 cm to 1 mile

Copyright of Geographers' A-Z Map Company Limited

Head Office:
Fairfield Road, Borough Green, Sevenoaks, Kent TN15 8PP
Telephone: 01732 781000 (Enquiries & Trade Sales)
01732 783422 (Retail Sales)
www.a-zmaps.co.uk
Copyright © Geographers' A-Z Map Co. Ltd.

Ordnance Survey This product includes mapping data licensed from Ordnance Survey® with the permission of the Controller of Her Majesty's Stationery Office.
© Crown Copyright 2005. All rights reserved. Licence number 100017302
Edition 3 2005

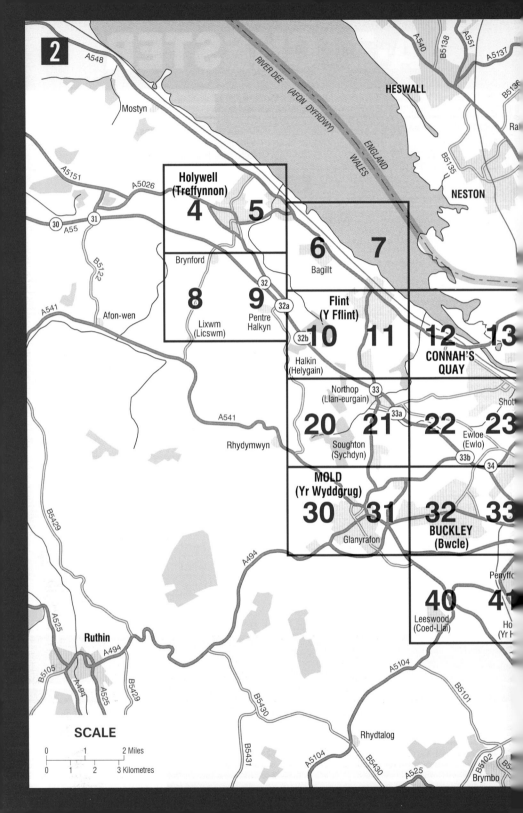

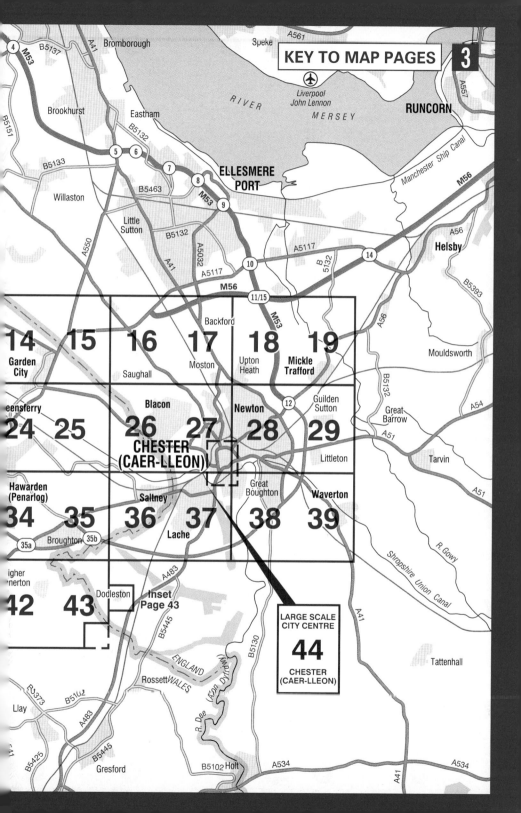

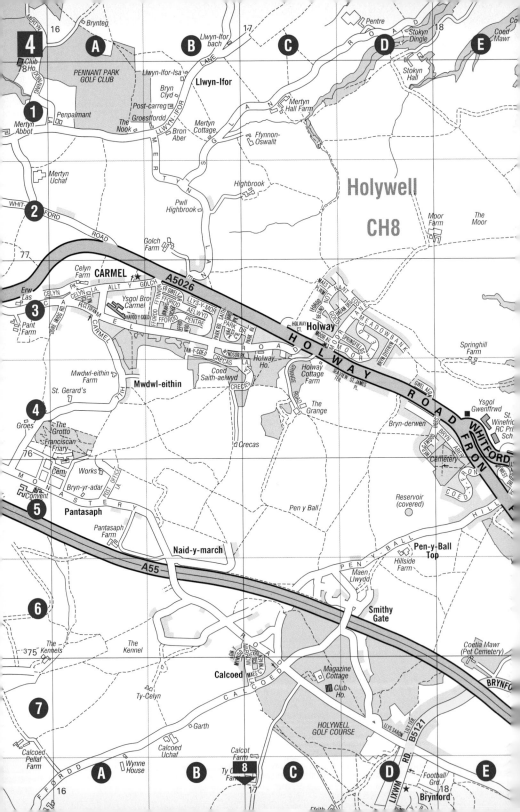

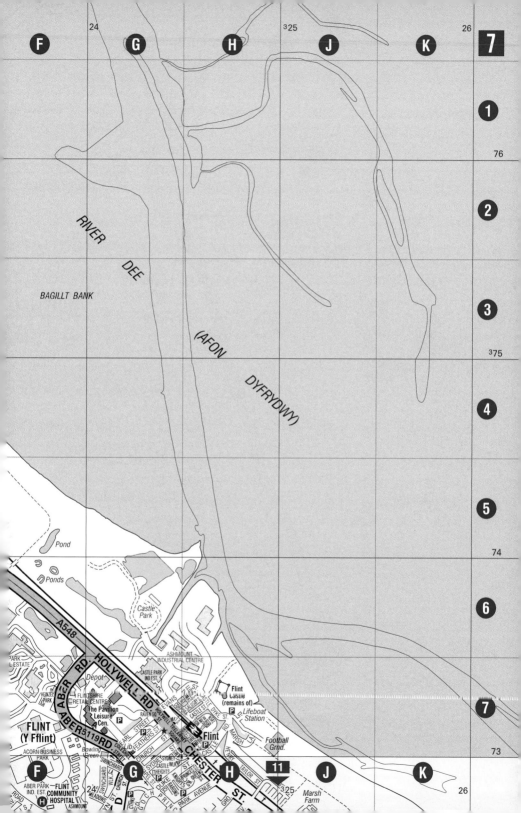

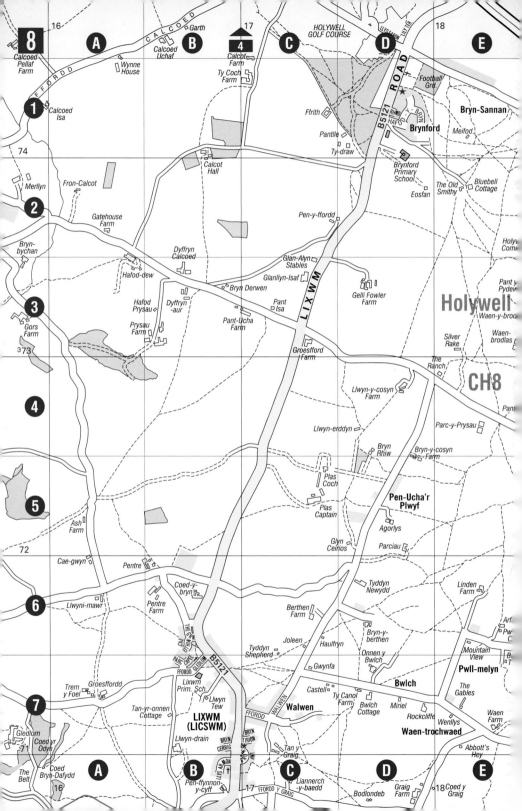

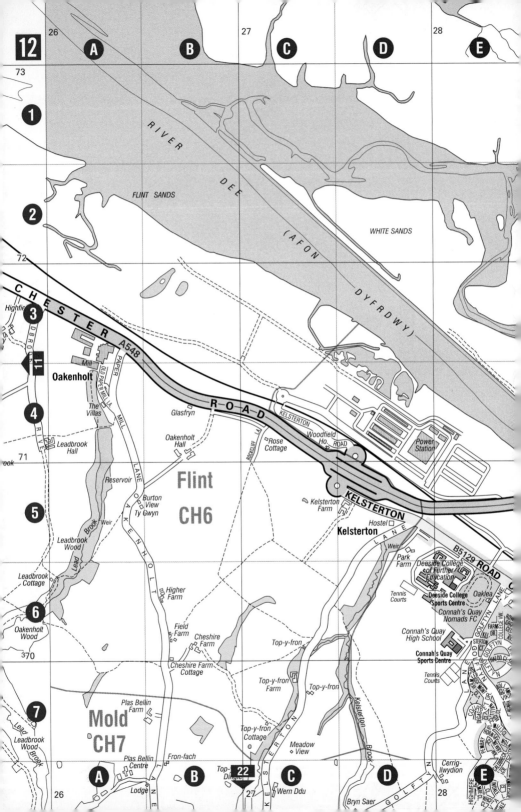

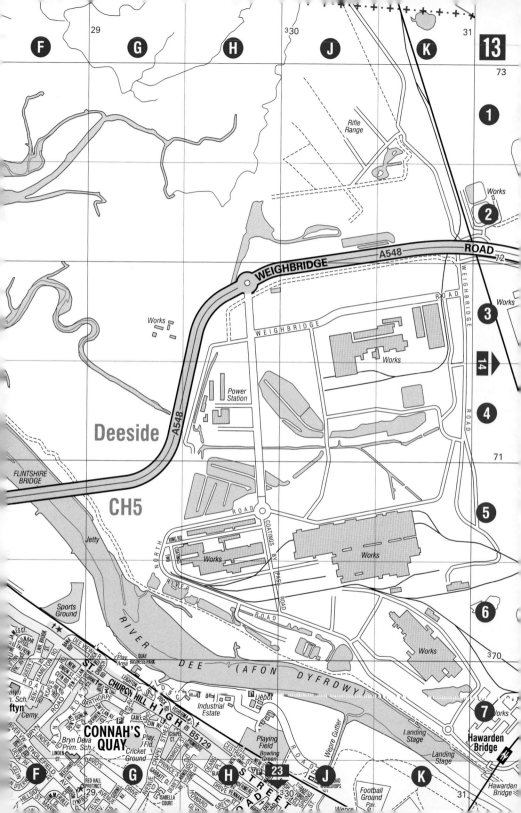

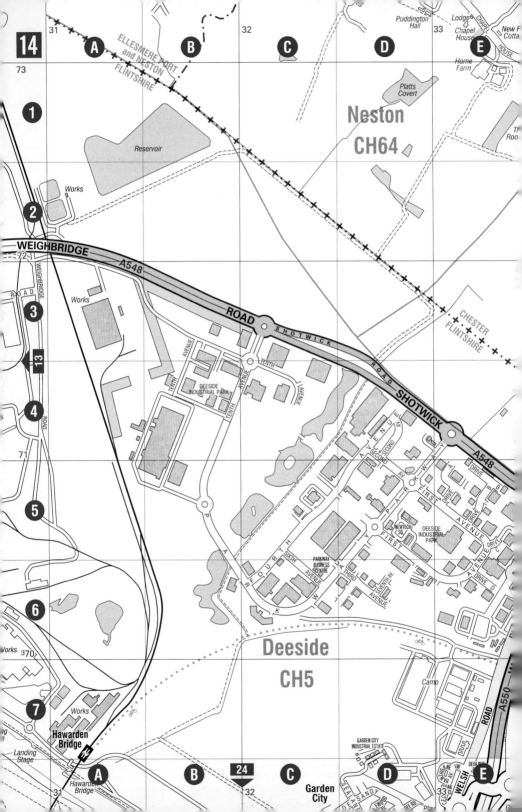

F 34 G H Showk Brook J PARKGATE K 36 **15**

The Remote

335 Twomills Farm

Corner Cottage

Rock Cottage

Delamare House

73

Woodbank

Rose Farm

1

Woodbank Hall

Pits Farm

A540

Shotwick Dale

Bryn Berllan

The Willows

Brookvale

Bank House

Daleside

Stack Polly

Hill View Farm

2

White Sails

The Paddocks

Roughwood Farm

Salcombe

Oakfield

72

Shotwick Hall Farm

Shotwick Dale Bridge

Park Farm

New Covert

◆ **Shotwick Hall**

Willow Cottage

hotwick

Council Holdings

he rage

Grange Farm

Four Ways

New Ways Farm

3

Woodbank Farm

SHOTWICK - HELSBY

A5117

BY-PASS

Shotwick Bridge

Hill View

Bleak Farm

Pleasant View Farm

West View

16

BIG WOOD

Lower Farm

Chester CH1

Wellfield Farm

Shotwicklodge Farm

4

71

Pool Garden Wood

Castle Farm

Shotwick Park Farm

5 Parkga Fe

Sports Field

Maes Gwyn

ENGLAND

WALES

Meadowbrook Cottage

Dingle Wood

Shotwick House

Shotwick Park

6

Camp

Meadow Brook Farm

Woodlands Farm

370

Greenfield Farm

CHURCH

GREEN LANE ESTATE

FOX

Bridge Farm

HERMITAGE RD

Morriston Farm

CROFTERS WAY

7

The Beeches

GREEN

Seahill Bridge

Coach House

BEECHES

Seahill Farm

F 34 G H **25** J K 36

335

Green Lane Farm

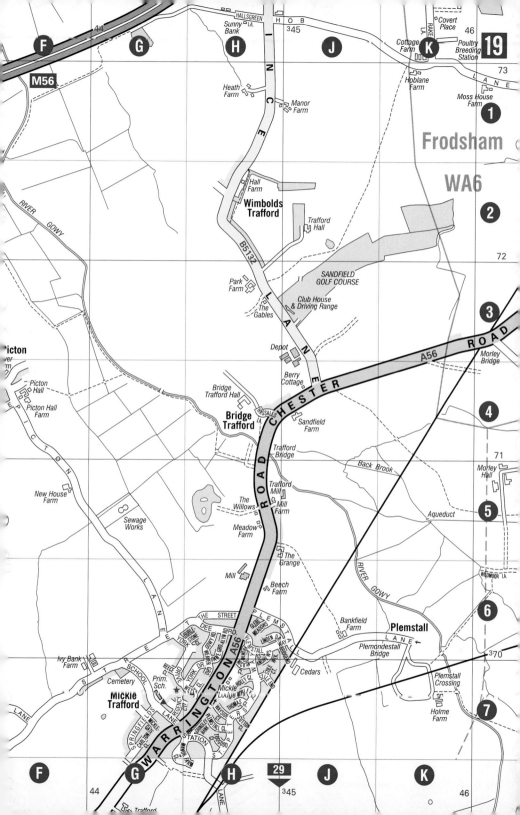

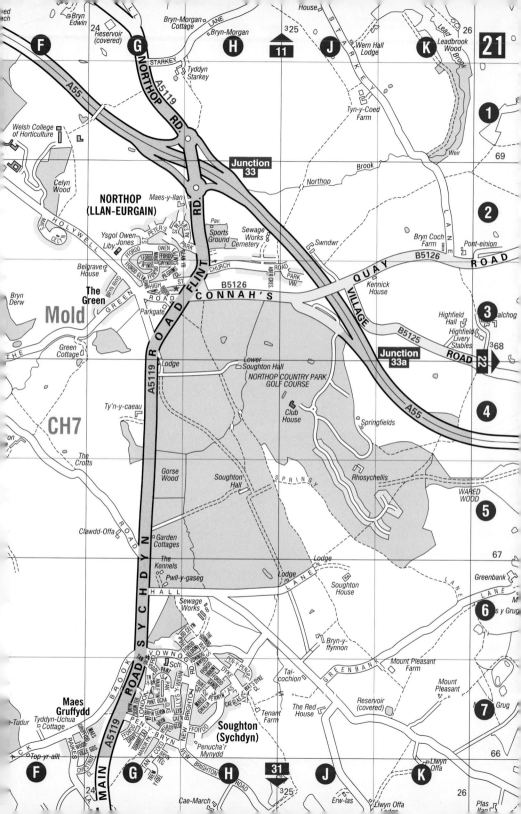

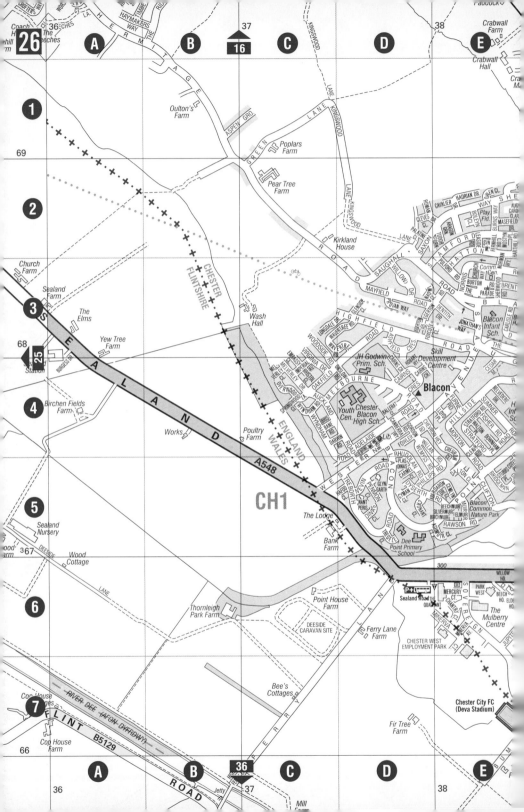

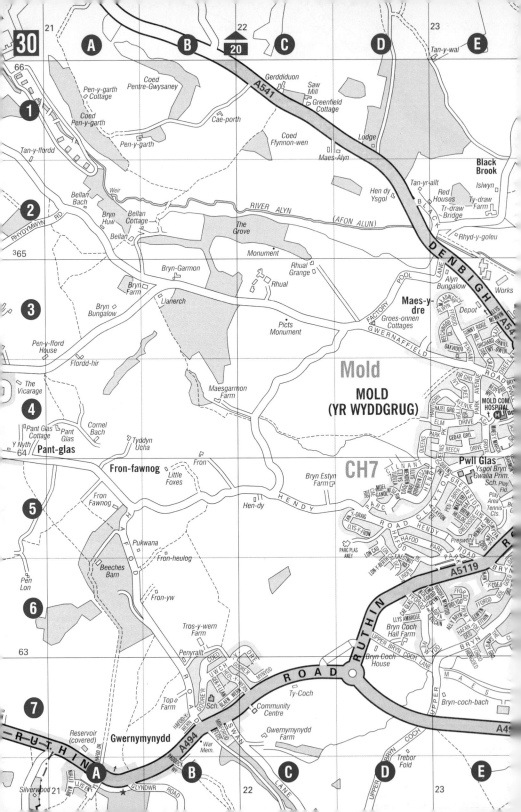

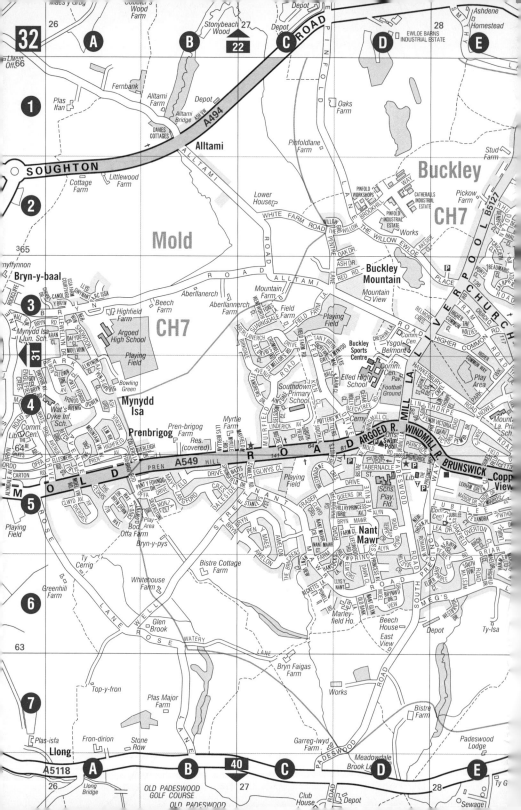

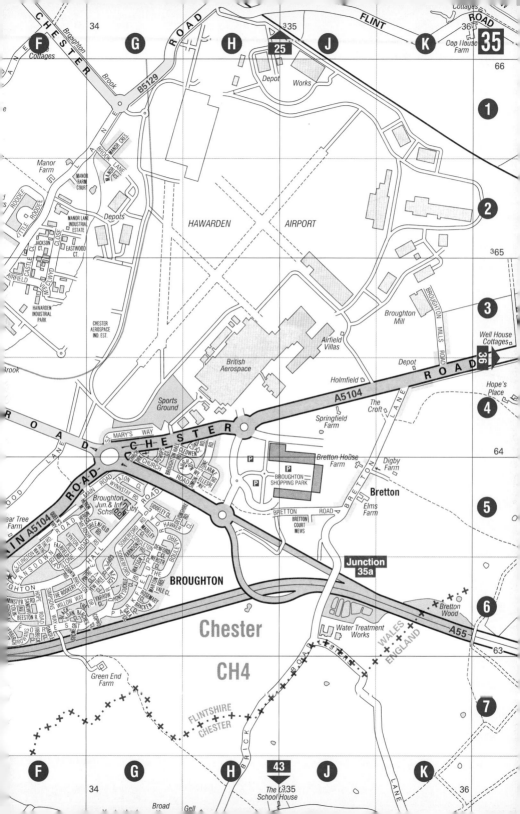

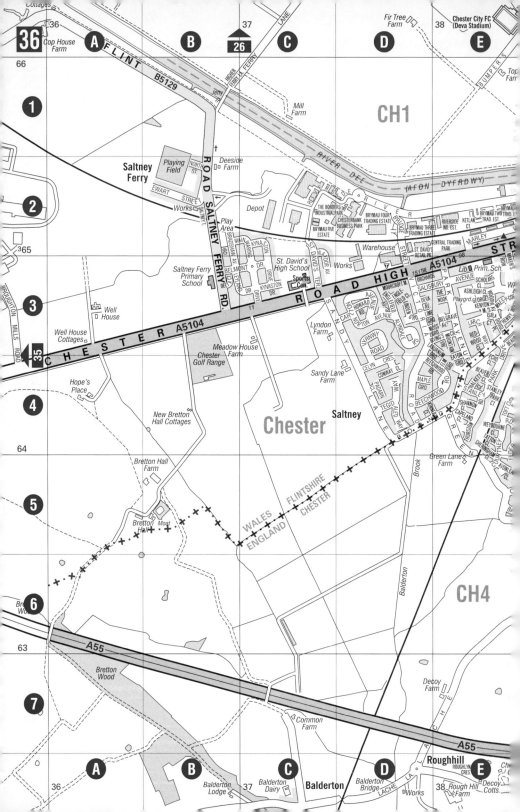

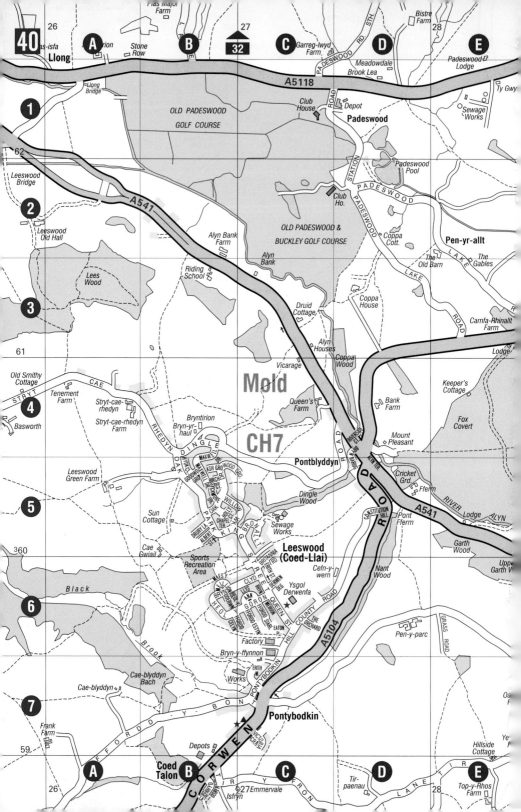

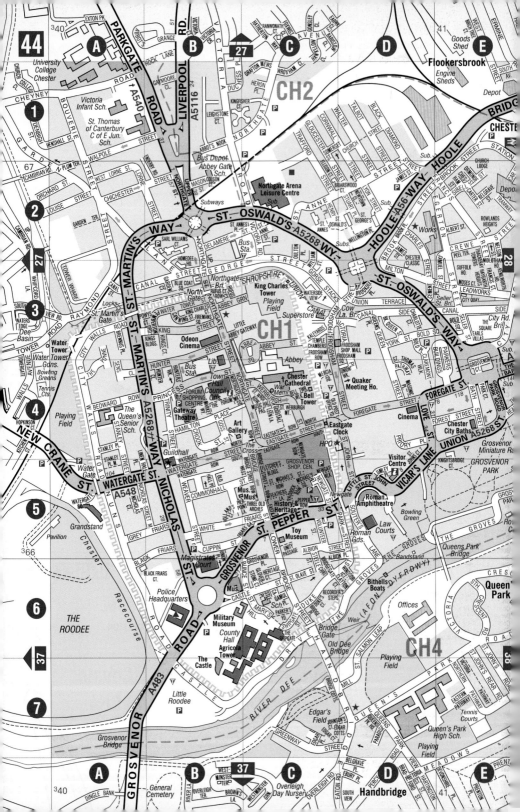

INDEX

Including Streets, Places & Areas, Hospitals & Hospices, Industrial Estates, Selected Flats & Walkways, Stations and Selected Places of Interest.

HOW TO USE THIS INDEX

1. Each street name is followed by its Postcode District and then by its Locality abbreviation(s) and then by its map reference; e.g. **Abbots Pk.** CH1: Ches . . . .4J **27** is in the CH1 Postcode District and the Chester Locality and is to be found in square 4J on page **27**. The page number is shown in bold type.

2. A strict alphabetical order is followed in which Av., Rd., St., etc. (though abbreviated) are read in full and as part of the street name; e.g. **Alderberry Rd.** appears after **Alder Av.** but before **Alder Gro.**

3. Streets and a selection of flats and walkways too small to be shown on the maps, appear in the index with the thoroughfare to which it is connected shown in brackets; e.g. **Ael-y-Ffynnon** CH8: Holy . . . .4E **4** (off Whitford St.)

4. Addresses that are in more than one part are referred to as not continuous.

5. Places and areas are shown in the index in BLUE TYPE and the map reference is to the actual map square in which the town centre or area is located and not to the place name shown on the map; e.g. **BOUGHTON** 7C **28**

6. An example of a selected place of interest is **Abbey Farm Mus.** 2G **5**

7. An example of a station is **Bache Station (Rail)** 3K **27**

8. An example of a hospital or hospice is COUNTESS OF CHESTER HOSPITAL 2H **27**

9. Map references shown in brackets; e.g. **Abbey Grn.** CH1: Ches . . . .6J **27** (3B **44**) refer to entries that also appear on the large scale page **44**.

GENERAL ABBREVIATIONS

App. : Approach	**Flds.** : Fields	**Pas.** : Passage
Av. : Avenue	**Gdns.** : Gardens	**Pl.** : Place
Bk. : Back	**Gth.** : Garth	**Pct.** : Precinct
Bri. : Bridge	**Ga.** : Gate	**Ri.** : Rise
Bldgs. : Buildings	**Grn.** : Green	**Rd.** : Road
Bungs. : Bungalows	**Gro.** : Grove	**Shop.** : Shopping
Bus. : Business	**Hgts.** : Heights	**Sth.** : South
Cvn. : Caravan	**Ho.** : House	**Sq.** : Square
Cen. : Centre	**Ind.** : Industrial	**St.** : Street
Cl. : Close	**Info.** : Information	**Ter.** : Terrace
Coll. : College	**La.** : Lane	**Twr.** : Tower
Comn. : Common	**Lit.** : Little	**Trad.** : Trading
Cotts. : Cottages	**Lwr.** : Lower	**Up.** : Upper
Ct. : Court	**Mdw.** : Meadow	**Vw.** : View
Cres. : Crescent	**Mdws.** : Meadows	**Vs.** : Villas
Cft. : Croft	**M.** : Mews	**Vis.** : Visitors
Dr. : Drive	**Mt.** : Mount	**Wlk.** : Walk
E. : East	**Mus.** : Museum	**W.** : West
Ent. : Enterprise	**Nth.** : North	**Yd.** : Yard
Est. : Estate	**Pde.** : Parade	
Fld. : Field	**Pk.** : Park	

LOCALITY ABBREVIATIONS

All : **Alltami**	Gard C : **Garden City**	Nor : **Northop**
Aston : **Aston**	Gt Bou : **Great Boughton**	Nor H : **Northop Hall**
Bab : **Babell**	G'fld : **Greenfield**	Oak : **Oakenholt**
Back : **Backford**	Guil S : **Guilden Sutton**	Pade : **Padeswood**
Bag : **Bagillt**	G'field : **Gwernaffield**	Pant : **Pantasaph**
Bald : **Balderton**	G'nydd : **Gwernymynydd**	Penf : **Penffordd**
Blac : **Blacon**	Halk : **Halkyn**	Pen : **Pentre**
Bret : **Bretton**	Hat H : **Hatton Heath**	Pen H : **Pentre Halkyn**
Bri T : **Bridge Trafford**	Haw : **Hawarden**	Penym : **Penymynydd**
Brou : **Broughton**	High K : **Higher Kinnerton**	Pic : **Picton**
B'ford : **Brynford**	Holw : **Holway**	Pont : **Pontblyddyn**
Bryn B : **Bryn-y-Baal**	Holy : **Holywell**	Ponty : **Pontybodkin**
Buck : **Buckley**	Hoole V : **Hoole Village**	Pudd : **Puddington**
Burt : **Burton**	Hope : **Hope**	Queen : **Queensferry**
Cae : **Caergwrle**	Hunt : **Huntington**	Rhes : **Rhes-y-cae**
Carm : **Carmel**	Kel : **Kelsterton**	Rhos : **Rhosesmor**
Cau : **Caughall**	Lea B : **Lea-by-Backford**	Row : **Rowton**
Ches : **Chester**	Lees : **Leeswood**	Saig : **Saighton**
Chor B : **Chorlton-by-Backford**	Lit B : **Little Barrow**	Salt : **Saltney**
Chris : **Christleton**	Lit S : **Little Stanney**	Salt F : **Saltney Ferry**
Coed : **Coed-talon**	L'ton : **Littleton**	Sand : **Sandycroft**
Con Q : **Connah's Quay**	Lixm : **Lixwm**	Saug : **Saughall**
Cot E : **Cotton Edmunds**	Llong : **Llong**	Sea : **Sealand**
C'ton : **Croughton**	Low K : **Lower Kinnerton**	Shot : **Shotton**
Dee I : **Deeside Industrial Park**	Man : **Mancot**	S'wck : **Shotwick**
Dob : **Dobshill**	Marl L : **Marlston-cum-Lache**	S'ton : **Soughton**
D'ton : **Dodleston**	Mick T : **Mickle Trafford**	Stoak : **Stoak**
Drury : **Drury**	Milwr : **Milwr**	Treu : **Treuddyn**
Dun H : **Dunham-on-the-Hill**	Mold : **Mold**	Upton : **Upton**
Dunk : **Dunkirk**	Moll : **Mollington**	Wav : **Waverton**
Ecc : **Eccleston**	Mos : **Moston**	Wer : **Wervin**
Ewl : **Ewloe**	M Isa : **Mynydd Isa**	Whit : **Whitford**
Flint : **Flint**	Nerc : **Nercwys**	Wim T : **Wimbolds Trafford**
Flint M : **Flint Mountain**	New B : **New Brighton**	Wood : **Woodbank**

A

	Abbey St. CH1: Ches 6K 27 (3C 44)	ABBOT'S MEADS 4J 27
	Abbey Vw. Trad. Est. CH8: G'fld 1H 5	Abbot's Nook CH2: Ches 5J 27 (1B 44)
Abbey Ct. CH8: G'fld 2G 5	Abbots Cl. CH6: Bag 4C 6	Abbots Pk. CH1: Ches 4J 27
Abbey Farm Mus. 2G 5	Abbots Ct. CH2: Ches 4J 27	Abbot's Ter. CH1: Ches 3H 27
Abbey Grn. CH1: Ches 6J 27 (3B 44)	Abbots Dr. CH2: Ches 4J 27	Abbots Wlk. CH8: Holy 4G 5
Abbey Sq. CH1: Ches 6K 27 (3C 44)	Abbot's Grange CH1: Ches 5J 27 (1A 44)	Abbotts Cl. CH3: Wav 4K 39
	Abbots Knoll CH1: Ches 4J 27	Abbottsford Dr. CH4: Penf 3H 41

Abbotts La. CH4: Penf .3H 41
    (not continuous)
Abbotts Rd. CH3: Wav 4K 39
Aber Cres. CH7: Nor .3H 21
Aberdaron Dr. CH1: Blac 5E 26
Aber Las CH6: Flint .3H 11
Aberllanerch Dr. CH7: Buck 3C 32
Aber Pk. Ind. Est. CH6: Flint 7F 7
    (Heinzel Pk.)
  CH6: Flint 1F 11
    (Old London Rd.)
Aber Rd. CH6: Flint 7F 7
Aber Vw. CH5: Con Q 7E 12
Abingdon Cres. CH4: Ches 3F 37
Acacia Cl. CH7: Mold 6G 31
Acorn Bus. Pk. CH6: Flint 7F 7
Acorn Cl. CH7: Buck 5G 33
Acorns, The CH2: Upton 7A 18
Acres La. CH2: Upton 6B 18
Adder Hill CH3: Gt Bou 2D 38
Adelaide Rd. CH1: Blac 4D 26
Adwy Wynt CH6: Flint 3H 11
Ael y Bryn CH7: Mold 6E 30
Ael-y-Ffynnon CH8: Holy 4E 4
    (off Whitford St.)
Afondale CH6: Flint .1F 11
Afon Vw. CH5: Con Q 7E 12
Agenora Cl. CH5: Con Q 7E 12
Agricola Tower 6B 44
Ainsdale Cl. CH7: Buck 4C 32
Airfield Vw. CH5: Haw 3F 35
Alamein Rd. CH2: Mos 6H 17
Albert Av. CH6: Flint 2H 11
Albert St. CH1: Ches 6A 28 (2E 44)
  CH7: Lees 5B 40
Albion M. CH1: Ches 5C 44
Albion Pl. CH1: Ches 7K 27 (5C 44)
Albion St. CH1: Ches 7K 27 (5C 44)
Alder Av. CH5: Aston 5J 23
Alderberry Rd. CH5: Haw 2H 33
Alder Gro. CH2: Ches 4D 28
Alderley Pl. CH1: Blac 2E 26
Alderney Ho. CH2: Ches 4D 28
Aldersey Cl. CH1: Saug 6A 16
  CH3: Hunt 7C 38
Aldford Rd. CH2: Upton 1B 28
Aled Cres. CH6: Flint 3F 11
Aled Ho. CH5: Ewl .7G 23
Aled Way CH4: Salt 4D 36
Alexander Ct. CH3: Ches 7A 28
    (off Dee La.)
Alexandra Ct. CH7: Buck 5E 32
Alexandra Rd. CH7: Mold 5F 31
Alexandra St. CH5: Shot 2K 23
Allans Cl. CH5: Shot 3A 24
Allansford Av. CH3: Wav 5J 39
Allerton Cl. CH4: Penf 1K 41
Allington Pl. CH4: Ches 2A 38
ALLTAMI 1B 32
Alltami Rd. CH7: All 1B 32
  CH7: Buck 3C 32
Allt Goch CH6: Flint 2G 11
Allt Goch La. CH7: Nor 7H 11
Allt y Golch CH8: Carm 3A 4
Allt-y-Plas CH8: Pen H 5H 9
Alma St. CH3: Ches 6B 28
Almond Way LL12: Hope 7K 41
Alpraham Cres. CH2: Upton 1A 28
Alun Cl. CH7: Nor H 4B 22
Alun Cres. CH4: Ches 3G 37
Alvis Rd. CH5: Sand 5F 25
Alwen Av. CH7: Bryn B 4A 32
Alwen Dr. CH5: Con Q 6G 23
  CH6: Bag 3A 6
Alwyn Cl. CH7: Mold 3E 30
Alwyn Gdns. CH2: Upton 7A 18
Alyndale Av. CH7: M Isa 5K 31
Alyndale Rd. CH4: Salt 3D 36
Alyn Dr. CH4: Penf .4J 41
Alyn Mdw. CH7: Mold 4F 31
Alyn Pk. CH5: Haw .1H 33
Alyn Rd. CH2: Mick T 6H 19
  CH7: Buck 5D 32
Alyn St. CH7: Mold .4G 31
Alyn Ter. CH7: Pont 5D 40
Ambleside CH2: Ches 2B 28
Ambleside Cl. CH5: Con Q 1E 22
Ambrose Lloyd Cen. CH7: Mold 5F 31
Anchorage, The CH3: Wav 4J 39
Andrew Cres. CH4: Ches 1A 38
Anfield Cl. CH5: Con Q 4F 23
Anne's Way CH4: Ches 1A 38
Anvil Cl. CH1: Saug 6A 16
Appleby Dr. CH5: Haw 6A 24
Appleton Rd. CH2: Upton 2A 28
Appleyards La. CH4: Ches 2K 37
Aragon Grn. CH1: Blac 2E 26
Aran Cl. CH7: Bryn B 3A 32
Archers Way CH1: Ches 6G 27
Archway CH7: Mold 6G 31
Arderne Ho. CH2: Upton 1B 28

Argoed Av. CH7: New B 2J 31
Argoed Bus. Pk. CH7: Mold 5G 31
Argoed Hall La. CH7: M Isa 5H 31
Argoed Rd. CH7: Buck 4D 32
Argoed Vw. CH7: New B 1J 31
Argyll Av. CH4: Ches 2G 37
Arkle Ct. CH3: Ches 6D 28
Arley Cl. CH2: Upton 2B 28
Arnhem Way CH3: Hunt 4D 38
Arnold Gro. CH5: Con Q 1H 23
Arnolds Cres. CH4: Brou 6E 34
Arradon Ct. CH2: Upton 3A 28
Arrowcroft Rd. CH3: Guil S 3H 29
Arthur St. CH1: Ches 6G 27
Ascot Ct. CH1: Ches 6H 27
    (off Sedgefield Rd.)
Ascot Ho. CH1: Ches 6H 27
Ash Bank CH3: Guil S 4E 28
Ashby Pl. CH2: Ches 5A 28
Ash Dr. CH7: Buck .3D 32
Ashfield Cres. CH1: Blac 3D 26
  CH5: Man 6B 24
Ashfield Rd. CH5: Shot 2K 23
Ash Gro. CH4: Ches 4H 37
  CH5: Shot 2K 23
  CH6: Flint 5E 6
  CH7: Lees 5B 40
  CH7: M Isa 4A 32
  CH7: Mold 4E 30
Ash Hey La. CH2: Pic 7E 18
Ash Ho. CH2: Ches 3J 27
Ash La. CH5: Man .7B 24
Ash Lawn Ct. CH2: Ches 4J 27
Ashlea Cl. CH5: Man 6B 24
Ashleigh Cl. CH4: Salt 3E 36
Ashmount Ent. Pk. CH6: Flint 1F 11
Ashmount Ind. Cen. CH6: Flint 6G 7
Ashmuir Cl. CH1: Blac 5E 26
Ashtree Ct. CH2: Ches 5A 28
Ash Vw. CH5: Aston 4J 23
  CH7: All 1B 32
Ashwood Cl. CH2: Ches 5C 28
Ashwood La. CH2: Wer 3C 18
Asiatic Cotts. CH5: Sand 5F 25
Aspen Cl. CH5: Con Q 1F 23
Aspen Gro. CH1: Saug 1B 26
Aspen Way CH2: Ches 4D 28
ASTON 5K 23
Aston Hill CH5: Aston 5K 23
  CH5: Ewl 5H 23
Aston Mead CH5: Aston 5K 23
Aston Pk. Rd. CH5: Aston 4J 23
Aston Rd. CH5: Queen 4K 23
Atis Cft. CH6: Flint .2J 11
Auckland Rd. CH1: Blac 4C 26
Auden Ct. CH5: Ewl 2G 33
Audley Cres. CH4: Ches 3K 37
Aughton Way CH4: Brou 5H 35
Augusta Ho. CH1: Blac 2E 26
Austen Cl. CH5: Ewl 1G 33
Avenue, The CH5: Haw 7A 24
  CH7: Mold 5G 31
Avon Cl. CH5: Con Q 2F 23
  CH7: Mold 6G 31
Avondale Rd. CH7: Buck 5F 33
Avonlea Cl. CH4: Ches 5E 36
Awel-y-Mor CH8: Holy 4H 5

B

Babbage Rd. CH5: Sand 4E 24
Bache Av. CH2: Upton 3J 27
Bache Dr. CH2: Ches 2K 27
Bachefield Av. CH3: Hunt 3C 38
Bache Hall Ct. CH2: Ches 3J 27
Bache Hall Est. CH2: Ches 3J 27
Bachelor's Ct. CH3: Gt Bou 1C 38
Bachelor's La. CH3: Ches, Gt Bou 1C 38
Bache Station (Rail) 3K 27
BACKFORD 3H 17
Back of Hoole La. CH2: Ches 6B 28
    (off Hoole La.)
Bk. Queen St. CH1: Ches 6K 27 (3D 44)
Badgers Cl. CH3: Chris 2G 39
Badgers Ri. CH5: Con Q 3F 23
Badgers Wlk. CH2: Cau 5A 18
Bagillt Rd. CH6: Bag 3K 5
  CH8: Bag, G'fld 1H 5
  CH8: Holy 5G 5
Bagillt St. CH8: Holy 5F 5
Bagillt Vw. CH8: Holy 4K 27
Bakers Ct. CH3: Ches 6A 28
    (off Steam Mill St.)
Bala Av. CH8: G'fld .2H 5
Bala Ho. CH5: Ewl .7H 23
BALDERTON 7C 36
Ballater Cres. CH3: Ches 6D 28
Ballerat Cl. CH1: Blac 4D 26
Balmoral Cl. CH6: Flint 1E 10

Balmoral Pk. CH1: Ches 5H 27
Bank Cl. CH2: Ches 3A 28
Bank La. CH7: Drury 3G 33
Bank Pl. CH8: Holy .5F 5
Bank Rd. CH5: Con Q 6F 13
Bank Row CH7: Buck 5F 33
Banks Rd. CH5: Man 7B 24
Bank Vs. CH7: Mold 4F 31
Bannel La. CH4: Penym 6G 33
  CH5: Dob 6J 33
  CH7: Buck 6G 33
Baristow Cl. CH2: Ches 5K 27 (1C 44)
Barkhill Rd. CH3: Ches 6C 28
Barley Cft. CH3: Gt Bou 2C 38
Barmouth Cl. CH5: Con Q 1E 22
Barnes Cl. CH1: Blac 2F 27
Barnyard, The CH5: Aston 5K 23
Barons Cl. CH6: Flint 1G 11
Barons Ct. CH2: Ches 4J 27
Barony Way CH4: Ches 5E 36
Barrel Well Hill CH3: Ches 7B 28
Bars, The CH3: Ches 7A 28 (4E 44)
Bartholomew Way CH4: Ches 3J 37
Bartlet Cl. CH7: Gard C 2C 24
Barwoods Dr. CH4: Ches 4E 36
Basingwerk Abbey .2H 5
Basingwerk Av. CH8: G'fld 1G 5
Bath St. CH1: Ches 7A 28 (4E 44)
Beaconsfield Rd. CH5: Shot 2J 23
Beaconsfield St. CH3: Ches 7A 28
Beaumaris Cl. CH7: Buck 3E 32
Beaumaris Rd. CH5: Con Q 1E 22
Beaumaris Saltney Sports Cen. 3C 36
Beaumont Cl. CH4: Salt 3E 36
Beaver Cl. CH4: Salt 4E 36
Becketts La. CH3: Ches, Gt Bou 1C 38
  CH7: Buck 6C 32
Bedford Way CH7: Mold 4E 30
Bedward Row CH1: Ches 7J 27 (4A 44)
Beechcroft Cl. CH6: Bag 3C 6
Beech Dr. CH7: Mold 4E 30
Beeches, The CH2: Upton 2B 28
  CH4: Salt F 7J 25
  CH5: Haw 2H 33
  CH8: Milwr 7F 5
  LL12: Hope 7K 41
Beeches La. CH1: Saug 7A 16
Beech Gro. CH2: Ches 5C 28
  CH7: M Isa 4A 32
Beech Ho. CH1: Ches 6E 26
Beechlands Av. CH3: Ches 7C 28
Beechmuir CH1: Blac 5E 26
Beech Rd. CH5: Aston 5J 23
  CH7: Drury 4H 33
Beechtree Rd. CH7: Buck 4D 32
Beechway CH2: Upton 2J 27
Beechwood Av. CH5: Con Q 1F 23
Beechwood Cl. CH7: Mold 3E 30
Beechwood Rd. CH4: Salt 4D 36
Beeston Pathway CH4: Ches 2A 38
Beeston Rd. CH4: Brou 6F 35
  CH4: High K 3E 42
Beeston Vw. CH4: Ches 2A 38
    (off Appleyards La.)
Belgrave Av. CH4: Salt 3E 36
Belgrave Cl. CH4: D'ton 7J 43
Belgrave Pl. CH4: Ches 2K 37 (7D 44)
Belgrave Rd. CH3: Gt Bou 1D 38
Belgrave St. CH1: Ches 6A 28 (2E 44)
Bellard Dr. CH2: Ches 4C 28
Bellevue La. CH3: Guil S 3G 29
Bell Tower 4C 44
Bell Twr. Wlk. CH1: Ches 7K 27 (4C 44)
Belmont Av. CH5: Con Q 2H 23
Belmont Cres. CH7: Buck 3D 32
Belmont Dr. CH4: Salt F 3B 36
Belvedere Cl. CH5: Queen 4E 26
Belvedere Dr. CH1: Blac 1E 22
Benllech Cl. CH5: Con Q 3D 42
Bennett's La. CH4: High K 6K 23
  CH5: Haw 6K 23
Bennett's Row CH6: Flint 3K 11
Benton Dr. CH2: Ches 4J 27
Berkley Cl. CH4: Ches 3A 38
Berkley Dr. CH4: Ches 3K 37
Bernsdale Cl. CH5: Sand 5D 24
Bernsdale Dr. CH5: Sand 5E 24
BERTH-DDU 1A 20
Berwyn Av. CH4: Penf 4J 41
Berwyn Cl. CH7: Bryn B 3A 32
  CH7: Buck 5E 32
Bethel Pl. CH5: Con Q 7G 13
Bewley Cl. CH3: Gt Bou 2C 38
Bidston Cl. CH2: Ches 3K 27
BIG MANCOT 6B 24
Bilberry Cl. CH4: Penf 1J 41
BILLINS 6G 5
Birch Cl. CH7: Buck .5E 32
Birch Ct. CH5: Con Q 7F 13
    (off New Union St.)
  CH7: Lees 5B 40

Birch Cft. CH5: Man 6C 24
Birches, The CH4: Brou 6F 35
Birchfield Cres. CH3: Aston 5K 23
Birch Heath La. CH3: Chris 1G 39
Birch Ho. CH1: Ches 3H 27
Birchmuir CH1: Blac 5E 26
Birch Ridge CH5: Flint 2E 10
Birch Ri. CH2: Ches 2K 27
    CH5: Haw 7K 23
Birch Rd. CH4: Ches 4F 37
Birch Tree Cl. CH2: Ches 5A 28 (1E 44)
Birkdale Av. CH7: Buck 3C 32
Bishops Ct. CH4: Brou 5G 35
Bishopsfield Ct. CH2: Ches 5B 28
    (off Derby Pl.)
Bishopsgate CH2: Ches 5C 28
Bishop St. CH2: Ches 5B 28
Bistre Av. CH7: Buck 5D 32
Bistre Cl. CH7: Buck 4C 32
Bithells Boats 1K 37 (6D 44)
BLACK BROOK .2E 30
Black Brook CH7: Rhos, S'ton 2D 30
Blackbrook Av. CH5: Haw 6A 24
Black Diamond St. CH1: Ches 5K 27 (1D 44)
Black Dog La. CH3: Wav 5J 39
Black Friars CH1: Ches 7J 27 (6A 44)
Black Friars Ct. CH1: Ches 6B 44
Blackthorn Cl. CH3: Hunt 4C 38
    CH4: Brou 6F 35
BLACON 4D 26
Blacon Av. CH1: Ches 3E 26
Blacon Common Nature Pk. 5E 26
Blacon Hall Rd. CH1: Blac 3F 27
Blacon Point Rd. CH1: Blac 5D 26
Blaen Wern CH7: G'nydd 7B 30
Blake Cl. CH1: Blac 2F 27
Blantern Rd. CH4: High K 3E 42
Blenheim Cl. CH5: Haw 7J 23
Blenheim Ho. CH1: Ches 5H 27
Bluebell Cl. CH3: Hunt 3D 38
Blue Coat Almshouses
    CH1: Ches 3B 44
Blue Coat Sq. CH1: Ches 6J 27 (3B 44)
Bodhyfryd CH6: Flint 1G 11
    (off Allt Goch)
Bodlondeb CH6: Flint 3H 11
Bodnant Gro. CH5: Con Q 2F 23
Bod Offa Dr. CH7: Buck 5A 32
Bold Pl. CH1: Ches 6K 27 (3D 44)
Bold Sq. CH1: Ches 6K 27 (3D 44)
Bolesworth Rd. CH2: Upton 2B 28
Boleyn Cl. CH1: Blac 2E 26
Bollam Cl. CH5: Con Q 7E 12
Bolland's Ct. CH1: Ches 7J 27 (5B 44)
Bollingbrooke Hgts. CH6: Flint 7G 7
    (off Earl St.)
BOOT END 4K 5
Borders Ind. Pk., The CH4: Salt 2C 36
Border Way CH3: Ches 7E 28
Borough Gro. CH6: Flint 1H 11
Bottoms La. CH4: Ches 1A 38
BOUGHTON 7C 28
Boughton CH3: Ches 7A 28
Boughton Cen., The CH3: Ches 6B 28
Boughton Hall Av. CH3: Ches 6G 35
Boughton Hall Dr. CH3: Gt Bou 7D 28
Boulevard, The CH4: Ches 6G 35
Boundary La. CH4: Salt 4D 36
Bouverie St. CH1: Ches 5J 27 (1A 44)
Bowery, The CH1: Sea 4H 25
Boxmoor Cl. CH4: Ches 4G 37
Boydell Way CH4: D'ton 7J 43
Bracken Cl. CH4: Brou 6G 35
Brackendale Rd. CH5: Queen 5B 24
Brackens, The CH7: Buck 6C 32
Bradford St. CH4: Ches 2K 37 (7D 44)
Bradshaw Av. CH4: Salt F 2B 36
Braemar Cl. CH4: Ches 5E 28
Braeside Av. CH5: Haw 6A 24
Bramble Cl. CH3: Gt Bou 2C 38
    CH7: Buck 6E 32
Brambles, The CH5: Shot 2K 23
    CH7: M Isa 4J 31
Bramley La. CH4: High K 3B 42
Bramley Way CH5: Ewl 1H 33
Brassey St. CH3: Ches 6B 28
Bray Rd. CH4: Ches 3F 37
Breeze Hill CH5: Con Q 1H 23
Brennus Pl. CH1: Ches 6J 27 (3A 44)
Brentwood Rd. CH1: Blac 2C 26
Breton Cl. CH2: Upton 3A 28
BRETTON 5J 35
Bretton Ct. M. CH4: Bret 5J 35
Bretton Dr. CH4: Brou 6F 35
Bretton La. CH4: Bret 5J 35
Bretton Rd. CH4: Bret 5J 35
Briar Dr. CH7: Buck 5E 32
Briarswood Ct. CH1: Ches 2D 44
Brickbarn Cl. CH1: Blac 4C 32
Brickfield La. CH3: L'ton 6H 29
Brickfields CH7: Buck 5F 33

Brick Rd. CH4: Low K 1H 43
Bricky La. CH3: Chris 7G 29
Bridge Cotts. CH4: Ches 1K 37 (7C 44)
Bridge Ct. CH3: Ches 6C 28
Bridge Dr. CH3: Chris 2F 39
Bridge Foyer, The CH1: Ches 6H 27
    (off Tower Rd.)
Bridgegate Chambers CH1: Ches . .1K 37 (6C 44)
Bridgeman Rd. CH1: Blac 5E 26
Bridgend CH2: Mick T 6J 19
Bridge Pl. CH1: Ches 1K 37 (6C 44)
Bridge St. CH1: Ches 7K 27 (5C 44)
    CH4: Salt 2D 36
    CH5: Shot 1J 23
    CH7: Mold 4G 31
Bridge St. Row E. CH1: Ches 4C 44
Bridge St. Row W. CH1: Ches 5C 44
Bridge Ter. CH3: Ches 6D 28
BRIDGE TRAFFORD 4H 19
Bridge Vw. CH5: Gard C 1D 24
Bridgewater Ct. CH2: Ches 6B 28
    (off Hoole La.)
Bridgewater Dr. CH3: Ches 6E 28
Brighton Ter. CH6: Bag 3K 5
    (off Bagillt Rd.)
Brisbane Rd. CH1: Blac 4C 26
Bristol Cl. CH1: Blac 4C 26
Britannia Rd. CH7: Lees 6C 40
Broadacre Cl. CH6: Bag 4C 6
Broadmead CH3: Ches 6E 28
Broad Oak Av. CH4: Brou 6E 34
Broad Oak Cl. CH5: Con Q 2F 23
Broadway CH5: Con Q 2G 23
    CH5: Ewl 6G 23
Broadway E. CH2: Ches 3A 28
Broadway W. CH2: Ches 3K 27
Bro Alun CH7: Mold 4F 31
Bro Deg CH6: Flint 2F 11
Brodie Cl. CH2: Mos 6J 17
Bromfield Cl. CH7: Mold 6G 31
Bromfield Ind. Est. CH7: Mold 6G 31
    (Queen's La., not continuous)
    CH7: Mold 7H 31
    (Stephen Gray Rd.)
Bromfield La. CH7: Mold 6G 31
Bromfield Pk. CH7: Mold 6G 31
Bronallt CH7: Lees 5C 40
Bronant CH8: Lixm 7C 8
Broncoed Bus. Pk. CH7: Mold 7G 31
Broncoed La. CH7: Mold 7F 31
    CH7: Mold 6G 31
Bron Haul CH6: Bag 4K 5
Bron Llwyn CH6: Flint 3H 11
Brongu Gro. CH5: Ewl 1G 33
Bron y Nant CH7: Mold 5G 31
Bro-yr-Eglwys CH7: M Isa 4J 31
Bron-y-Wern CH6: Bag 4B 6
Brook Ct. CH1: Ches 5H 27
    (off Cheyney Rd.)
Brookdale Av. CH5: Con Q 2G 23
Brookdale Pl. CH1: Ches 2F 11
Brookdale Pl. CH1: Ches 6K 27 (3D 44)
Brookdale Way CH3: Wav 4K 39
Brooke Av. CH2: Upton 7B 18
Brooke Cl. CH5: Ewl 1G 33
Brookes Av. CH4: Brou 6F 35
Brookfield Dr. CH2: Ches 4A 28
Brookhill Way CH7: Buck 2D 32
Brook La. CH2: Ches 5J 27
    CH5: Haw 1G 35
Brookleigh Av. CH5: Man 6B 24
Brookmore Ct. CH2: Ches 5J 27
    (off Brook La.)
Brook Mt. CH7: Mold 5F 31
Brook Pl. CH1: Ches 6K 27 (2D 44)
Brookside CH3: Gt Bou 1C 38
    CH5: Gard C .2J 23
    CH7: Nor H 4B 22
Brookside Cres. CH7: Nor H 4B 22
Brookside Ter. CH2: Ches 5K 27
Brook St. CH1: Ches 6K 27 (2D 44)
    CH7: Buck 5F 33
    CH7: Mold 5F 31
    CH7: Nor 3G 21
    (off Holywell Rd.)
BROUGHTON 6F 35
Broughton Hall Rd. CH4: Brou 6F 35
Broughton Mills Rd. CH4: Bret 3K 35
Draughton Shop. Pk. CH4: Brou 5J 35
BROWN HEATH .3K 39
Brown Heath Rd. CH3: Chris, Wav 2J 39
Browning Cl. CH1: Blac 2F 27
Brown's La. CH4: Ches 2J 37 (7B 44)
Browns Pl. CH5: Sand 5E 24
Brownsway CH8: Holy 4F 5
Brunswick Rd. CH7: Buck 5D 32
    (not continuous)
Brunswood Grn. CH5: Haw 1H 33
Brushwood Av. CH6: Flint 2E 10
Bryan Gro. CH7: M Isa 4K 31

Brymau Five Est. CH4: Salt 2C 36
Brymau Four Trad. Est. CH4: Salt 2D 36
Brymau One Trad. Est. CH4: Salt 2E 36
Brymau Three Trad. Est. CH4: Salt 2D 36
Brymau Two Trad. Est. CH4: Salt 2E 36
Bryn Aber CH6: Bag 4C 6
    CH8: Holy 4E 4
Bryn Aelwyd Ucha CH8: Carm 3B 4
Bryn Afon CH8: G'fld 2F 5
Bryn Arnold CH5: Con Q 1H 23
Brynawel CH8: Pen H 4H 9
Bryn Awelon CH6: Flint 3H 11
    (off Moel Parc)
    CH7: Buck 5B 32
    CH7: Mold 3G 31
Bryn Barug CH7: Pont 4D 40
Bryn Cae Pl. CH5: Con Q 7G 13
BRYN CELYN 3F 5
Bryn Cerrig CH8: Lixm 7B 8
Bryn Clwyd CH7: M Isa 3K 31
Bryn Clyd CH7: Lees 6B 40
Bryn Coch Cres. CH7: Mold 6E 30
Bryn Coch La. CH7: Mold 6E 30
Bryn-Coed-Wepre CH5: Con Q 4E 22
Bryn Derw CH6: Flint 3H 11
Bryn Derwen CH7: M Isa 5A 32
Bryn Dr. CH5: Haw 6A 24
Bryn Dyffry CH8: Holw 4D 4
Bryn Dyrys CH6: Bag 4C 6
Bryn Eglwys CH6: Flint M 6G 11
Bryn Eithin CH5: Con Q 3E 22
    CH7: G'nydd .7A 30
    CH8: Pen H 5H 9
Brynemlyn CH8: Pen H 5J 9
Bryn Felin CH8: Pen H 4H 9
BRYNFORD 1D 8
Brynford Hill CH8: B'ford 7E 4
Brynford Rd. CH8: Holy, B'ford 7F 5
    CH8: Pen H 4G 9
Brynford St. CH8: Holy 5F 5
Bryn Garmon CH7: Mold 4E 30
Bryn Glas CH6: Flint 2F 11
Bryn Gwyn CH6: Flint 3H 11
Bryn-Gwyn La. CH7: Nor, Nor H 3C 22
Bryn Helyg CH6: Flint 3H 11
Bryn Heulog CH7: Mold 5E 30
Bryn Hilyn La. CH7: Mold 6G 31
Bryn Hytryd CH5: Con Q 2E 22
    CH7: S'ton 7G 21
Bryn La. CH7: New B 2J 31
Bryn Mawr CH7: Buck 5D 32
Bryn Mawr Rd. CH8: Holy 4F 5
Bryn Meirion CH7: Lees 6C 40
Bryn Mor Dr. CH6: Flint 2F 11
Bryn Noddfa CH7: Mold 4E 30
Bryn Offa CH7: M Isa 5J 31
Bryn Onnen CH6: Flint 3H 11
Bryn Rhyd CH7: Nor 3G 21
Bryn Rd. CH5: Con Q 7F 13
    CH6: Flint 2G 11
    CH7: All, Bryn B 3K 31
    (not continuous)
    CH7: M Isa 5K 31
BRYN-SANNAN .1E 8
Bryn Seion La. CH7: S'ton 7G 21
Bryn Seion Ter. CH7: S'ton 7G 21
Bryn Siriol CH6: Flint 2H 11
Bryn Teg CH7: S'ton 7G 21
    CH8: Holy 4H 5
Bryn Tirion CH8: Lixm 7C 8
Bryntirion Rd. CH6: Bag 4C 6
    (Neston Vw.)
    CH6: Bag 5C 6
    (Trebor Av.)
Brynwood Dr. CH7: Buck 6D 32
BRYN-Y-BAAL 3K 31
Bryn-y-Baal Rd. CH7: Bryn B 3K 31
Bryn-y-Coed CH8: Holy 4F 5
Bryn-y-Felin CH8: Holy 4F 5
Bryn-y-Foel CH7: Rhos 2A 20
BRYN-Y-GARREG 7E 10
Bryn-y-Gwynt CH8: Holy 4G 5
    CH8: Pen H 5J 9
Buckingham Av. CH3: Ches 6D 28
BUCKLEY (BWCLE) 5D 32
BUCKLEY MOUNTAIN 3D 32
Buckley Sports Cen. 3D 32
Buckley Station (Rail) 6H 33
Buckley Swimming Pool 4D 32
Bulkeley St. CH3: Ches 6C 28
Bumper's La. CH1: Ches 1E 36
Bunce St. CH1: Ches 1K 37 (6C 44)
Burgess Dr. CH1: Sea 4A 26
Burges St. CH2: Ches 5B 28
Burnham Rd. CH4: Ches 3F 37
Burns Cl. CH5: Ewl 2G 33
Burns Way CH1: Blac 2E 26
Burntwood Ct. CH7: Drury 3G 33
BURNTWOOD PENTRE 3G 33
Burntwood Rd. CH7: Drury 3G 33
Burton Ct. CH5: Con Q 1F 23

Burton Dr. CH4: High K 3D 42
Burton Rd. CH1: Blac 3E 26
Bush Rd. CH3: Chris 2G 39
Butler St. CH5: Shot 3K 23
Butterbache Rd. CH3: Hunt 3B 38
Butterbur Cl. CH3: Hunt 3C 38
Buttermere Cl. Con Q 1E 22
Buxton La. CH8: Pen H 4G 9
BWLCH 7D 8
Bye Pass, The CH3: L'ton 6G 29
Byron Cl. CH1: Blac 2E 26
   CH5: Con Q 3F 23
   CH5: Ewl 1G 33
Bythom Cl. CH3: Chris 2G 39

C

Cable St. CH5: Con Q 7G 13
Cadnant Cl. CH1: Blac 5D 26
Cadnant Ct. CH4: Brou 4H 35
Cadnant Dr. CH6: Bag 3B 6
Cae Berwyn CH7: S'ton 7H 21
Cae Bracty CH7: Mold 5F 31
Cae Bychan CH6: Flint 3H 11
Cae Derw CH6: Flint 2H 11
   CH8: Pen H 4H 9
Cae Eithin CH8: Lixm 6B 8
Cae Fawnog CH4: Penf 3J 41
Cae Glas CH7: Mold 6D 30
   CH7: S'ton 7H 21
Cae Gwenith CH8: G'fld 2F 5
Cae Haf CH7: Nor H 4C 22
Cae Helyg CH8: Pen H 4H 9
Cae Hir CH6: Flint 2H 11
   CH7: Mold 5D 30
Cae Isa CH7: New B 1J 31
Cae Llys Cl. CH5: Con Q 3E 22
Cae Masarn CH8: Pen H 5H 9
Cae-Mefus CH8: Holy 5E 4
Cae Petit CH6: Flint 2H 11
Cae'r Ffynnon CH6: Bag 4K 5
   CH7: Rhos 3A 20
Cae'r Fron CH8: Holy 6F 5
Caernarvon Cl. CH5: Shot 3K 23
Caer Onnen CH8: Pen H 4H 9
Caerphilly Rd. CH7: Buck 3E 32
Cae'r Rhos CH7: Rhos 3A 20
Caesar Av. CH6: Flint 2J 11
Cae-y-Dderwen CH8: G'fld 2F 5
Cairndale Av. CH5: Con Q 1F 23
Cairns Cres. CH1: Blac 4D 26
Cairnton Cres. CH8: G'fld 2H 5
CALCOED 7C 4
Caldbreck Cres. CH5: Con Q 1E 22
Caldy Av. CH5: Con Q 2F 23
Caldy Cl. CH2: Ches 3K 27
Caldy Valley Rd. CH3: Hunt, Gt Bou 3C 38
Cambrian Av. CH3: Ches 6D 28
Cambrian Cl. CH5: Con Q 1G 23
   CH7: Mold 7G 31
Cambrian Ct. CH1: Ches 6H 27
Cambrian Rd. CH1: Ches 6H 27 (2A 44)
Cambrian Vw. CH1: Ches 5H 27
            (off Whipcord La.)
Cambrian Way CH5: Ewl 6J 23
Cambridge Rd. CH2: Ches 3B 28
Campion Cl. CH3: Hunt 3C 38
Camrose CH5: Con Q 4D 22
Canadian Av. CH2: Ches 4C 28
Canal Side CH1: Ches 6K 27 (3D 44)
Canal St. CH1: Ches 6J 27 (3A 44)
Canberra Way CH1: Blac 4D 26
Canning St. CH1: Ches 6J 27 (3B 44)
Cannon Way CH4: High K 4D 42
Canol y Bryn CH7: Bryn B 3A 32
Canon Dr. CH6: Bag 5C 6
Canterbury Rd. CH1: Blac 3F 27
Capeland Cl. CH4: Salt 4E 36
Capel y Nant CH7: Nor 3G 21
            (off Holywell Rd.)
Capesthorne Rd. CH3: Chris 4J 39
Carlines Av. CH5: Ewl 6H 23
Carlisle Rd. CH1: Blac 3E 26
Carlton Av. CH4: Salt 3D 36
Carlton Cl. CH2: Mick T 7G 19
Carlton Pl. CH2: Ches 4C 28
CARMEL 3A 4
Carmel Cl. CH1: Blac 5D 26
Carmel Hill CH8: Carm 3A 4
Carmel Rd. CH8: Carm, Holw 3A 4
Caroline Ho. CH1: Blac 2E 26
Carrick Rd. CH4: Ches 1G 37
Car St. CH1: Ches 6A 28 (2E 44)
Carter St. CH1: Ches 6A 28 (2E 44)
Carton Rd. CH7: M Isa 5K 31
Castle, The 1J 37 (7B 44)
Castle Cl. CH5: Haw 3F 35
Castle Cft. Rd. CH4: Ches 4H 37
Castle Dr. CH1: Ches 1J 37 (7B 44)

Castle Dyke St. CH6: Flint 7H 7
Castle Hgts. CH6: Flint 1G 11
Castle Hill St. CH5: Shot 4K 23
Castlemere Cl. CH4: Brou 6E 34
Castle M. CH5: Shot 2J 23
Castle Pk. Av. CH5: Con Q 3E 22
Castle Pk. Ind. Est. CH6: Flint 7G 7
Castle Pl. CH1: Ches 1K 37 (6C 44)
Castle Ri. CH5: Haw 1B 34
Castle Rd. CH6: Flint 7H 7
Castle St. CH1: Ches 1J 37 (6B 44)
   CH6: Flint 7H 7
   CH7: Mold 5F 31
            (off New St.)
Castle Way CH4: D'ton 7J 43
Cathcart Grn. CH3: Guil S 3H 29
            (off Oaklands)
Catheralls Ind. Est. CH7: Buck 2D 32
Catherine Dr. CH5: Ewl 6J 23
Catherine St. CH1: Ches 6H 27
Caughall Rd. CH2: Cau 4A 18
   CH2: Upton 7A 18
Cavalier Dr. CH1: Blac 2E 26
Cavendish Rd. CH4: Ches 4D 28
Cawdor Dr. CH3: Ches 6C 28
Cecil St. CH3: Ches 7G 7
Cedar Av. CH5: Con Q 6E 12
   CH5: Gard C 1E 24
Cedar Cl. CH5: Gard C 1E 24
   CH7: Buck 4D 32
Cedar Ct. CH5: Con Q 7F 13
            (off Church St.)
Cedar Dr. CH2: Ches 4D 28
Cedar Gdns. CH5: Aston 5J 23
Cedar Gro. CH5: Ches 4D 28
   CH7: Mold 4E 30
Cedar M. CH1: Blac 4E 26
Cedars, The CH7: M Isa 5A 32
Cefna Cl. CH5: Con Q 3E 22
Cefn Eurgain La. CH7: Nor, Rhos 5A 20
Cefn La. CH6: Bag 1H 9
   CH8: Milwr 1H 9
Cefn Rd. CH5: Con Q 7F 13
Celandine Cl. CH3: Hunt 2C 38
Celtic St. CH5: Con Q 1J 23
Celyn Av. CH5: Con Q 1G 23
Celyn Cl. CH8: Carm 3A 4
Celyn Cres. CH4: Salt 4D 36
Celyn La. CH8: Carm 3A 4
Celyn Pk. CH8: Carm 3A 4
Cement Pl. CH1: Ches 6A 28 (3D 44)
Cemlyn Cl. CH1: Blac 5E 26
Central Dr. CH5: Shot 3K 23
Central Trad. Pk. CH4: Salt 2E 36
Cestrian St. CH5: Con Q 7H 13
Chain Maker's Row CH4: Salt 3E 36
Chambers La. CH7: Bryn B, M Isa 5K 31
Chancel Dr. CH6: Bag 5C 6
Chandos Cl. CH4: Ches 3A 38
Channel, The CH2: Back 3H 17
Chantry Ct. CH1: Ches 6E 26
   CH3: Row 4J 39
Chapel Cl. CH3: Saug 6A 16
Chapel Ct. CH5: Con Q 7G 13
Chapel Ho. La. CH64: Pudd 1E 14
Chapel La. CH3: Ches 7C 28
   CH7: M Isa 5K 31
Chapel St. CH5: Ches 6A 28
   CH5: Con Q 1G 23
   CH6: Flint 1G 11
   CH7: Mold 5F 31
Chapel Ter. CH7: Lees 5B 40
Chapel Wlk. CH7: S'ton 7G 21
            (off London Rd.)
Charles Cres. CH4: Ches 1A 38
Charles Dr. CH6: Flint 2H 11
Charles Rd. CH2: Mos 7H 17
Charles St. CH1: Ches 6K 27 (2D 44)
   CH2: Ches 5B 28
   CH7: Mold 7F 31
Charlotte Ct. CH1: Ches 6A 28 (3D 44)
Charlotte St. CH1: Ches 6H 27
Charmleys La. CH5: Shot 3J 23
            (Griffiths Ct.)
   CH5: Shot 2K 23
            (Brambles, The)
Charterhall Dr. CH2: Ches 6B 28
Chase, The CH4: High K 3D 42
Chaser Ct. CH1: Ches 5F 27
Chatsworth Dr. CH2: Ches 3C 28
Chatsworth Ho. CH1: Ches 5H 27
Chaucer Cl. CH1: Blac 2E 26
   CH5: Ewl 2G 33
Chelford Cl. CH1: Ches 7F 27
Chelford M. CH3: Ches 6D 28
            (off Pearl La.)
Chemistry La. CH5: Pen 4C 24
Cheriton Cl. CH5: Con Q 3E 22
Cherry Dale Rd. CH4: Brou 6D 34

Cherry Dr. CH7: Bryn B 3K 31
Cherry Gdns. CH3: Ches 7C 28
Cherry Gro. Rd. CH3: Ches 7C 28
Cherry Orchard Rd. CH4: Brou 3B 34
   CH5: Haw 3B 34
Cherry Rd. CH3: Ches 7C 28
Chesham St. CH1: Ches 6A 28 (2E 44)
Cheshire County Sports Club 2B 28
Cheshire La. CH7: Buck 3D 32
Cheshire Vw. CH4: Ches 2A 38
CHESTER (CAER-LLEON) 7K 27 (4C 44)
Chester Aerospace Ind. Est. CH5: Haw 3G 35
Chester Aerospace Pk. CH5: Haw 3E 34
Chester App. CH4: Ches 3J 37
Chesterbank Bus. Pk. CH4: Salt 2D 36
Chester Bus. Pk. CH4: Ches 6J 37
            (Kingsfield Ct.)
   CH4: Ches 6H 37
            (Sandpiper Way)
Chester Cathedral 7K 27 (4C 44)
Chester City Baths 7A 28 (4E 44)
Chester City FC 7E 26
Chester Classic CH1: Ches 2D 44
Chester Cl. CH5: Shot 3K 23
Chester Crematorium CH1: Ches 4G 27
Chester Ent. Cen. CH2: Ches 5A 28
Chester Gates CH1: Dunk 1D 16
Chester Gates Ind. Pk. CH1: Dunk 2D 16
Chester Heritage Cen. 7K 27 (5C 44)
Chester La. CH3: Saig 7F 39
Chester Racecourse 1H 37 (7A 44)
Chester Retail Pk. CH1: Ches 5G 27
Chester Rd. CH1: Back 1F 17
   CH2: Bri T 4J 19
   CH3: Hunt 2C 38
   CH4: Bret, Brou, Salt F 4G 35
   CH4: Penf, Penym 2J 41
            (not continuous)
   CH4: Penym 7K 33
   CH4: Salt F 6E 24
   CH5: Dob 5K 33
   CH5: Haw 1C 34
   CH5: Pen, Sand, Haw 4B 24
   CH6: Flint, Oak 1J 11
   CH7: Buck 5F 33
   CH7: Mold 4G 31
   WA6: Dun H 4J 19
Chester Rd. E. CH5: Pen 4B 24
   CH5: Queen 3B 24
   CH5: Shot 2K 23
Chester Rd. W. CH5: Queen 3A 24
   CH5: Shot 1J 23
Chester Station (Rail) 6A 28
Chester St. CH4: Salt 2F 37
   CH6: Flint 7H 7
   CH7: Mold 5F 31
Chesterton Av. CH5: Con Q 1G 33
Chesterton Ct. CH2: Ches 4K 27
Chester W. Employment Pk.
   CH1: Ches 6D 26
Chester Zoo 6A 18
Chestnut Cl. CH2: Ches 5C 28
   CH6: Flint 2F 11
   CH7: S'ton 1F 31
Chestnut Ct. CH5: Con Q 7F 13
            (off New Union St.)
Chestnut Cres. CH5: Haw 2H 33
Chestnut Gro. CH5: Haw 6A 24
Chestnut Rd. CH7: Mold 5D 30
Chevron Cl. CH1: Blac 4E 26
Chevron Hey CH1: Blac 4D 26
Chevrons Ct. CH5: Shot 3K 23
Chevrons Rd. CH5: Shot 3K 23
Cheyney Rd. CH1: Ches 5H 27 (1A 44)
Chichester St. CH1: Ches 6J 27 (2A 44)
Chiltern Cl. CH4: Ches 4H 37
   CH5: Con Q 2F 23
Chirk Cl. CH2: Upton 2B 28
Chorlton La. CH2: Chor B 1H 17
CHRISTLETON 1G 39
Christleton Rd. CH3: Ches 7B 28
Church Cl. CH7: Buck 3E 32
   CH7: Nor H 4B 22
   CH8: G'fld 1G 5
Church Coll. Cl. CH1: Ches 5H 27 (1A 44)
Church Cft. CH4: D'ton 7J 43
Church Hall Cl. CH1: Blac 4F 27
Church Hill CH5: Con Q 7G 13
Churchill Cl. CH5: Haw 1J 33
Church La. CH2: Back 3H 17
   CH2: Upton 1K 27
   CH3: Guil S 4H 29
   CH5: Ewl 5H 23
   CH5: Haw 1B 34
   CH5: Mold 4F 31
Church Lodge CH1: Ches 1E 44
Church Rd. CH1: Saug 6A 16
   CH4: Bald, D'ton 6J 43
   CH4: Brou 5G 35
   CH4: Ecc 7A 38
   CH5: Con Q 7G 13

Church Rd. CH7: Buck 3E 32
  CH7: Nor 3H 21
Church St. CH1: Ches 5K 27 (1D 44)
  CH5: Con Q 6E 12
  CH6: Flint 1G 11
Church Ter. CH8: Rhes 7F 9
Church Vw. CH5: Pen 5D 24
Church Wlk. CH4: Brou 5G 35
  CH6: Bag 4C 6
Church Walks CH3: Chris 1G 39
Churchward Cl. CH2: Ches 4K 27
Churton Rd. CH3: Ches 3E 26
Churton St. CH3: Ches 6C 28
Churton St. CH3: Ches 6C 28
Cilfan CH6: Flint 1F 11
                (off Maes-y-Coed)
Cilnant CH7: Mold 5D 30
Cinder Cl. CH3: Guil S 3H 29
Cinder La. CH3: Guil S 4H 29
Circuit Raceway, The 4F 25
Circular Dr. CH4: Ches 5E 36
  CH5: Ewl 6G 23
City Quay CH1: Ches 3E 44
City Rd. CH1: Ches 6A 28 (3E 44)
City Walls Rd. CH1: Ches 6J 27 (3A 44)
Clair Av. CH5: Sand 5E 24
Clare Av. CH2: Ches 5B 28
Clare Ho. CH1: Blac 2E 26
Claremont Av. CH5: Gard C 2C 24
Claremont Wlk. CH1: Ches 7K 27 (4D 44)
Clarence Av. CH3: Ches 6D 28
Clarence St. CH5: Shot 3K 23
Clarendon Cl. CH4: Ches 3A 38
Claverton Ct. CH4: Ches 1A 38 (6E 44)
Clay Hill La. CH5: Queen 4A 24
Claypit Rd. CH4: Ches 4H 37
Claypits La. CH3: Row 4H 39
Clayton Cl. CH1: Ches 1K 37 (6D 44)
  CH7: Mold 5E 30
Clayton Rd. CH7: Mold 5D 30
Cleaver Rd. CH1: Blac 4E 26
Cledwen Dr. CH7: Bryn B 4A 32
Cledwen Rd. CH4: Brou 4H 35
Cleveland Gro. CH5: Gard C 2C 24
Cleves Cl. CH1: Blac 2D 26
Clifford Dr. CH4: Ches 4F 37
Clifton Dr. CH1: Blac, Ches 5E 26
Clifton Pk. Av. CH5: Con Q 7F 13
Cliveden Rd. CH4: Ches 5F 37
Clivedon Rd. CH5: Con Q 2F 23
Clos Coed CH5: Pen 4C 24
Close, The CH1: Saug 6A 16
  CH5: Haw 7J 23
  CH7: Mold 6E 30
  CH8: G'fld 1G 5
Clos y Capel CH7: Buck 4D 32
Clos y Meillion CH5: Ewl 1G 33
Clover La. CH4: Ches 4F 37
Clover Pl. CH4: Ches 4F 37
Clwyd Av. CH7: M Isa 5A 32
  CH8: G'fld 3H 5
Clwyd Cl. CH5: Haw 3F 35
Clwyd Cres. CH7: New B 2J 31
                (not continuous)
Clwyd Gro. CH7: Buck 5C 32
Clwyd St. CH5: Shot 4K 23
Clwyd Theatre (Theatr Clwyd) 2G 31
Clydesdale Rd. CH7: Drury 4H 33
Clydfan CH8: Carm 3A 4
Coalpit La. CH1: Dunk 1E 16
  CH1: Lea B 2E 16
  CH1: Moll 4C 16
Coatings By-Pass Rd.
  CH5: Dee I 5H 13
Coatings Two CH5: Dee I 5G 13
Cobbles, The CH4: Ches 2K 37
Coed Bach CH6: Flint 2F 11
Coed Onn Rd. CH6: Flint 2G 11
COED TALON 7B 40
Coed Terfyn CH4: Penym 7J 33
Coed y Bryn CH6: Flint M 6G 11
Coed-y-Fron CH8: Holy 5E 4
Coed y Graig CH4: Penym 1J 41
Colchester Sq. CH4: Ches 4F 37
Colehill Pl. CH5: Con Q 6F 13
Coleridge Cl. CH1: Blac 3G 27
Coleshill Fechan CH6: Bag 5D 6
Coleshill Lea CH6: Flint 7G 7
                (off Coleshill St.)
Coleshill St. CH6: Flint 7G 7
  CH8: Holy 5F 5
Colinwood Av. CH4: Brou 6F 35
College Grn. CH4: Ches 2K 37
College Vw. CH5: Con Q 6E 12
Colliers La. CH7: M Isa 4A 32
Colliery La. CH5: Man 5B 24
Colson Ct. CH1: Ches 2B 44
Coltsfoot Cl. CH3: Hunt 4C 38
Columbine Cl. CH3: Hunt 4C 38
Commonhall St. CH1: Ches 7J 27 (5B 44)
Common La. CH3: Wav 4J 39

Compton Pl. CH4: Ches 3G 37
Congleton Rd. CH4: Brou 5G 35
Coniston Cl. CH5: Con Q 2E 22
Coniston Dr. CH7: Buck 4E 32
Coniston Rd. CH2: Ches 2B 28
CONNAH'S QUAY 1J 23
Connah's Quay Rd. CH7: Nor 3H 21
Connah's Quay Sports Cen. 6D 12
Connah's Quay Swimming Pool 2J 23
Connaught Av. CH5: Shot 2K 23
Constitution Hill CH7: Pont 5D 40
Conway Av. CH7: Buck 6F 33
Conway Cl. CH4: Salt 4D 36
  CH6: Flint 3F 11
Conway Ct. CH5: Con Q 1E 22
Conway St. CH7: Mold 6F 31
Coopers Cft. CH3: Gt Bou 2C 38
Cooper's La. CH5: Con Q 6F 13
Copeswood Cl. CH4: Brou 6G 35
Coppack Cl. CH5: Con Q 3E 22
Coppafield Cl. CH7: Buck 5F 33
COPPA VIEW 5F 33
Copper Beech Cl. CH4: Brou 6G 35
Coppergate, The CH5: Haw 7A 24
Coppice, The CH5: Ewl 6H 23
Coppins Cl. CH3: Ches 6C 28
Copse, The CH5: Haw 1H 33
CORK 4D 22
Cornist Dr. CH6: Flint 1F 11
Cornist La. CH6: Flint 1B 10
Cornist Rd. CH6: Flint 1F 11
Cornwall Rd. CH2: Upton 1B 28
  CH5: Shot 3K 23
Cornwall St. CH1: Ches 5K 27 (1C 44)
Coronation Rd. CH4: Brou 6F 35
Coronation St. CH4: Salt 2F 37
Corporation St. CH6: Flint 7G 7
Corun y Bryn CH5: Con Q 3E 22
Corwen Cl. CH5: Con Q 2E 22
Corwen Rd. CH5: Pen 3J 41
  CH7: Pont, Coed, Ponty 7B 40
Corwen Way CH4: Penf 3J 41
Cotebrook Dr. CH2: Upton 1A 28
Cotes Pl. CH1: Blac 5E 26
Cotgreave Cl. CH4: Ches 4H 37
Cotswold Cl. CH2: Upton 2B 28
Cotswold Cl. CH3: Ches 7C 28
Cottage Gdns. CH7: Buck 5F 33
Cottage La. CH5: Man 6B 24
Cottage Rd. CH4: Ches 4H 37
Cotterill Cl. CH4: Ches 3F 23
Countess Ct. CH1: Ches 3H 27
COUNTESS OF CHESTER HOSPITAL 2H 27
Countess Way CH1: Ches 4H 27
County Ct. Pl. CH8: Holy 5F 5
               (off Brynford St.)
County Rd. CH7: Lees 6C 40
Courbet Dr. CH5: Con Q 7E 12
Courtland Dr. CH5: Aston 4J 23
Courtney Rd. CH4: Ches 5E 36
Courtyard, The CH5: Shot 2A 24
Cousens Way CH1: Ches 4H 27
Cowhey Cl. CH4: Ches 4H 37
Cowthorne Dr. CH3: Wav 4J 39
Crabwall Pl. CH1: Blac 3F 27
Craithie Rd. CH3: Ches 6C 28
Cranbrook Cl. CH5: Con Q 2G 23
Crane Bank CH1: Ches 7H 27
Crane Wharf CH1: Ches 7H 27
Cranford Ct. CH4: Ches 4G 37
Cranleigh Cres. CH1: Ches 4H 27
Crawford's Wlk. CH2: Ches 5B 28
Crecas La. CH8: Carm 4B 4
Crescent, The CH2: Ches 4K 27
Crewe St. CH1: Ches 6A 28 (2E 44)
Criccieth Cl. CH7: Buck 2E 32
Croes Atti La. CH6: Flint 2J 11
Croft, The CH2: Ches 3K 27
  CH5: Aston 5K 23
Croft Av. CH5: Con Q 2G 23
Croft Cl. CH3: Row 4J 39
Crofters Pk. CH5: Sand 5E 24
Crofters Way CH1: Saug 7K 15
  CH5: Man 6C 24
Crompton Cl. CH5: High K 3D 42
Cromwell Av. CH7: Buck 3C 32
Cromwell Cl. CH4: Penf 2J 41
  CH5: Haw 7J 23
Crookenden Cl. CH2: Mos 6J 17
Crookenden Rd. CH2: Mos 6J 17
Crook St. CH1: Ches 7J 27 (4B 44)
Crosfield Dr. CH8: G'fld 2F 5
Cross, The CH7: Buck 4D 32
  CH7: Mold 5F 31
Cross Grn. CH2: Upton 2A 28
Cross Hey CH4: Ches 1A 38
Cross Keys CH7: Rhos 2A 20
Crossley Cres. CH2: Ches 3D 28
Cross Roads CH8: Holy 5F 5

Cross St. CH2: Ches 6B 28
  CH8: Holy 5F 5
Cross Tree Cl. CH5: Haw 1B 34
Cross Tree Ct. CH7: Buck 1F 33
Cross Tree La. CH5: Haw 7B 24
Crossway CH5: Ewl 6H 23
Crossways CH4: Penf 1J 41
  CH5: Man 5C 24
  CH5: Shot 3K 23
CROUGHTON 2B 18
Croughton Rd. CH2: C'ton 1B 18
  CH2: Stoak 1C 18
Crud-y-Gwynt CH7: M Isa 5A 32
Cunliffe St. CH7: Mold 6F 31
Cuppin St. CH1: Ches 7J 27 (5B 44)
Curzon Cl. CH5: Haw 1H 37
CURZON PARK 2G 37
Curzon Pk. Nth. CH4: Ches 1H 37
Curzon Pk. Sth. CH4: Ches 2G 37
Curzon St. CH4: Salt 2F 37
Cwm Cl. CH7: M Isa 5K 31
Cwm Eithin CH6: Flint 3H 11
Cwrt Brenig CH7: Buck 5F 33
Cwrt Cable CH5: Con Q 7G 13
                (off High St.)
Cwrt Onnen CH5: Man 7C 24
Cwrt Telford CH5: Con Q 3F 23
             (Hazelwood Cl.)
CH5: Con Q 2F 23
         (off Hollowbrook Dr.)
Cyman Cl. CH1: Blac 5D 26

D

Dafydd Cl. CH7: Bryn B 3A 32
Daisy Hill Rd. CH7: Buck 5E 32
DALE, THE 6H 17
Dale Dr. CH2: Upton 7K 17
Dale Rd. CH5: Aston 4J 23
Daleside CH2: Upton 7K 17
  CH7: Buck 5B 32
Dale St. CH3: Ches 7C 28
Dalton Cl. CH1: Blac 5E 26
Dane Cl. CH4: Ches 4F 37
Dane Gro. CH2: Mick T 6H 19
Daniell Way CH3: Gt Bou 2C 38
Daniel Owen Pct. CH7: Mold 5F 31
Darlington Cres. CH1: Saug 6A 16
Darwen Dr. CH4: Penym 1K 41
Darwin Rd. CH1: Ches 4C 26
Daulwyn Rd. CH7: Drury 3G 33
Dauncey Cl. CH2: Mos 6J 17
Davies Cotts. CH7: All 1B 32
Dawn Cl. CH7: Buck 6D 32
Dawpool Cl. CH2: Ches 3K 27
Dawson Dr. CH1: Ches 5J 27
Daytona Dr. CH7: Nor H 4C 22
Ddol Awel CH7: Mold 5D 30
Ddre Iniog Rd. CH8: Carm 3A 4
Deanery Cl. CH1: Ches 4J 27
Dean's Av. CH5: Con Q 1G 23
Deansbury Cl. CH6: Flint 1E 10
Deans Cl. CH2: Upton 2K 27
  CH6: Bag 5C 6
Deans Pl. CH5: Con Q 1H 23
Deans Way CH4: High K 2E 42
Dee Bank Ind. Est. CH6: Bag 1A 6
Dee Banks CH3: Ches, Gt Bou 1B 38
Dee Cotts. CH6: Flint 1H 11
Dee Fords Av. CH3: Ches 7C 28
Dee Hills Pk. CH3: Ches 7A 28
Dee La. CH3: Ches 7A 28 (4E 44)
Dee Rd. CH2: Mick T 6H 19
  CH5: Con Q 2H 23
  CH5: Gard C 1D 24
Deeside Cvn. Site CH1: Ches 6C 26
Deeside College Sports Cen. 6E 12
DEESIDE COMMUNITY HOSPITAL 4K 23
Deeside Ct. CH3: Ches 7A 28
Deeside Cres. CH1: Sea 3J 25
Deeside Ent. Cen. CH5: Shot 2A 24
Deeside Ent. Pk. CH5: Shot 2A 24
Deeside Ind. Pk. CH5: Dee I 5D 14
               (Newtech Sq.)
  CH5: Dee I 5B 14
                 (Tenth Av.)
Deeside La. CH1: Sea 4H 25
             (not continuous)
Deeside Leisure Cen. 3B 24
Dee Vw. CH5: Shot 4A 24
Dee Vw. Rd. CH5: Con Q 6F 13
  CH8: G'fld 2G 5
Deganwy Cl. CH7: Buck 2E 32
Degas Cl. CH5: Con Q 7E 12
Deinoil's Rd. CH5: Man 6C 24
Delamere Av. CH7: Buck 6F 33
Delamere St. CH1: Ches 6J 27 (2B 44)
Dell, The CH3: Guil S 3H 29
Delta Cl. CH4: Salt 3B 36
Delves Wlk. CH3: Gt Bou 2D 38

Delvine Dr. CH2: Upton 2K 27
Delyn Rd. CH8: G'fld 2F 5
Demage La. CH1: Lea B 3F 17
   CH2: Upton 7K 17
Demage La. Sth. CH2: Upton 1K 27
Denbigh Cl. CH7: Buck 2E 32
Denbigh Rd. CH7: Mold 2E 30
Denbigh St. CH1: Ches 5H 27 (1A 44)
Denford Cl. CH4: Brou 5G 35
Denhall Cl. CH2: Ches 3A 28
Dennis Dr. CH4: Ches 3H 37
Denson Dr. CH5: Ewl 6J 23
Denstone Dr. CH4: Ches 5G 37
Dentith Dr. CH1: Blac 3E 26
Derby Pl. CH2: Ches 5A 28
Derby Ter. CH8: G'fld 2J 5
Derwen Cl. CH5: Con Q 7G 13
Derwen Deg CH7: Lees 6C 40
Derwent Rd. CH2: Ches 3B 28
Deva Av. CH4: Salt 3D 36
   CH5: Con Q 7F 13
   CH8: Holy 4F 5
Deva Bus. Pk. CH5: Gard C 1E 24
Deva Cl. CH6: Flint 2J 11
Deva Ct. CH2: Ches 6B 28
Deva Hgts. CH3: Gt Bou 2B 38
Deva La. CH2: Ches 2J 27
Deva Link CH1: Ches 5G 27
Deva Roman Experience 5B 44
Deva Stadium 7E 26
Deva Ter. CH3: Ches 7A 28
Devon Cl. CH5: Con Q 2F 23
Devon Rd. CH2: Ches 3B 28
Devonshire Pl. Ches 2A 38 (7A 44)
Devonshire Rd. CH4: Brou 5G 35
Dewi Av. CH8: Holy 5E 4
Dicksons Dr. CH2: Ches 3K 27
Dig La. CH5: Haw 1C 34
Dinas Cl. CH1: Blac 5D 26
Dinghouse CH7: Drury 2G 33
Dinghouse Wood CH7: Drury 3G 33
Dingle Bank CH4: Ches 2J 37 (7A 44)
Dingle Rd. CH7: Lees, Pont 4B 40
Dirty Mile CH5: Dob 5H 33
   CH7: Buck 5H 33
Disraeli Cl. CH5: Haw 1H 33
DOBS HILL 5J 33
DOBSHILL HOSPITAL 6H 33
Dock Rd. CH5: Con Q 7G 13
   CH8: G'fld 1H 5
Dock Rd. Workshops CH5: Con Q 1J 23
Dodds Ct. CH5: Shot 4J 23
Dodd's Dr. CH5: Con Q 1H 23
DODLESTON 6J 43
Dol Awel CH5: Ewl 7H 23
DOLPHIN 2H 9
Dolphin Ct. CH4: Ches 2G 37
Donne Pl. CH1: Blac 2F 27
Donnington Way CH4: Salt 2F 37
Dorchester Rd. CH4: Ches 4F 37
Dorfold Way CH2: Upton 2A 28
Dorin Ct. CH2: Upton 2K 27
Dormer Cl. CH3: Row 4J 39
Dorset Pl. CH2: Ches 3C 28
Dorset Rd. CH2: Upton 1B 28
Douglas Pl. CH4: Salt 3E 36
Dover Rd. CH4: Ches 3G 37
Dovey Cl. CH5: Con Q 2F 23
   CH6: Flint 3F 11
Downham Pl. CH1: Blac 4E 26
Downsfield Rd. CH4: Ches 3F 37
Downswood Ct. CH1: Ches 4J 27
Downswood Dr. CH1: Ches 4J 27
Dragons Health Club 3J 37
Dreflan CH7: Mold 4E 30
Drive A CH5: Dee I 5E 14
Drive B CH5: Dee I 5E 14
Drive C CH5: Dee I 5E 14
Drive D CH5: Dee I 6E 14
Drome Rd. CH5: Dee I 5E 14
DRURY 4H 33
Drury La. CH5: Haw 4F 33
   CH7: Buck, Drury 4F 33
   CH7: Lees 5B 40
Drury La. Ind. Est. CH7: Drury 3G 33
Drury New Rd. CH7: Drury 4G 33
Dryden Cl. CH5: Ewl 1G 33
Dryersfield CH3: Ches 1C 38
Duchess Pl. CH2: Ches 5J 27 (1B 44)
Duckers La. CH5: Haw, Man 6C 24
Duffryn CH7: Buck 5F 33
Duke's Ct. CH1: Ches 6C 44
Dukesfield Cl. CH7: Buck 5E 32
Duke's Fld. Dr. CH7: Buck 5E 32
Duke St. CH1: Ches 1K 37 (6C 44)
   CH6: Flint 1G 11
   CH7: S'ton 7H 21
Dukesway CH2: Upton 1A 28
Duke Wlk. CH6: Flint 1G 11
                 (off Duke St.)
Dulas Ct. CH2: Upton 7A 18

Dulverton Av. CH3: Ches 6E 28
Dunbar Cl. CH5: Con Q 6F 13
Dundas St. CH5: Queen 3B 24
Dunham Way CH2: Upton 2B 28
DUNKIRK 1E 16
Dunkirk La. CH1: Dunk 1D 16
Dunkirk Trad. Est. CH1: Dunk 1E 16
Dunlin Av. CH5: Con Q 7F 13
Durban Av. CH3: Chris 2F 39
Durham Rd. CH1: Blac 3E 26
Duttons La. CH7: Upton 7C 18
Dwyfor Av. CH7: Bryn B 4K 31
Dyfed Dr. CH5: Queen 4B 24
Dylan Cl. CH5: Ewl 2G 33
Dyserth Rd. CH1: Blac 5D 26

E

Eardswick Cl. CH2: Ches 5K 27 (1C 44)
Earles Cres. CH5: Man 5C 24
Earl Rd. CH7: Mold 5F 31
Earls Lea CH6: Flint 7G 7
                 (off Earl St.)
Earls Oak CH2: Upton 1K 27
Earl's Port CH1: Ches 6H 27
           (off South Vw. Rd.)
Earlston Ct. CH3: Ches 7A 28
Earl St. CH6: Flint 7G 7
Earls Vs. CH1: Ches 3E 44
Earlsway CH4: Ches 2G 37
East Cl. CH7: M Isa 5J 31
Eastern Pathway CH4: Ches 1K 37 (7E 44)
Eastfields Gro. CH1: Saug 7A 16
Eastgate Clock 7K 27 (4C 44)
Eastgate Row Nth. CH1: Ches 7K 27 (4C 44)
Eastgate Row Sth. CH1: Ches 4C 44
Eastgate St. CH1: Ches 7K 27 (4C 44)
East Grn. CH5: Sea 2E 24
East Vw. CH7: New B 2J 31
Eastwood Ct. CH5: Haw 2F 35
Eaton Av. CH4: Ches 2K 37
   CH5: Con Q 2H 23
Eaton Cl. CH4: Brou 5G 35
Eaton Gro. CH4: Salt 4E 36
Eaton M. CH4: Ches 2K 37
Eaton Pl. CH7: Lees 6C 40
Eaton Rd. CH4: Ches, Ecc 2K 37 (7C 44)
Ebury Pl. CH4: Ches 2K 37 (7D 44)
ECCLESTON 7A 38
Eccleston Av. CH4: Ches 3K 37
Eccleston Rd. CH4: High K 3E 42
Echo Cl. CH4: Salt 4E 36
Edgar Cotts. CH4: Ches 7C 44
Edgar Ct. CH4: Ches 7C 44
Edgar Pl. CH4: Ches 1K 37 (7C 44)
Edge Gro. CH2: Ches 6B 28
Edinburgh Way CH4: Ches 1A 38
Edmund St. CH7: Mold 6F 31
Edna St. CH2: Ches 5B 28
Edwards Rd. CH4: Ches 3G 37
Edwin Dr. CH6: Flint 2H 11
Egerton Dr. CH2: Ches 3K 27
Egerton M. CH1: Ches 3E 44
          (off Leadworld La.)
Egerton Rd. CH1: Blac 3D 26
Egerton St. Ches 6A 28 (2E 44)
Egerton Wlk. CH4: D'ton 6J 43
Eggbridge La. CH3: Wav 4J 39
Eglwys Cl. CH7: Buck 5C 32
Eirlys Gdns. CH7: M Isa 5A 32
Elder Dr. CH4: Ches 4E 36
Elder Ho. CH1: Ches 6E 26
Elfed Dr. CH7: Buck 5C 32
Elgin Cl. CH3: Ches 5C 28
Elidie Cl. CH5: Con Q 7E 12
Eliot Cl. CH5: Ewl 1G 33
Elizabeth Cres. CH4: Ches 7A 28
Ellesmere Av. CH2: Ches 3K 27
   CH4: Brou 5H 35
Ellesmere Rd. CH7: M Isa 5A 32
Ellison Ct. CH1: Ches 2C 44
Elm Av. CH5: Con Q 1F 23
   CH6: Flint 1F 11
Elm Cft. CH5: Man 6C 24
Elm Dr. CH7: Mold 4E 30
   CH7: Nor H 4B 22
Elm Gro. CH4: Salt 4E 36
   CH7: Buck 6D 32
Elm Ho. CH2: Ches 3H 27
Elm Rd. CH5: Aston 5J 23
Elms, The CH5: Haw 2H 33
Elm Sq. CH4: Ches 3F 37
Elmuir CH1: Blac 5E 26
Elm Wlk. CH7: M Isa 4A 32
Elm Way CH5: Ewl 6G 23
Elmwood Av. CH2: Ches 4B 28
Elmwood Cl. CH5: Shot 4K 23
Elstree Av. CH3: Ches 5D 28
Elwy Cl. CH7: Bryn B 4A 32
Elwy Cres. CH6: Flint 3F 11

Embassy Cl. CH1: Blac 4C 26
Enderby Rd. CH1: Ches 6J 27 (2B 44)
END LANE 5G 33
Endsleigh Cl. CH2: Upton 7A 18
Endsleigh Gdns. CH2: Upton 7A 18
Engineer Pk. CH5: Sand 4E 24
Englefield Av. CH4: Salt 3D 36
   CH5: Con Q 7F 13
Englefield Cres. CH7: M Isa 4K 31
Englefield Dr. CH6: Flint 2J 11
Englefield Rd. CH8: G'fld 1G 5
Ennerdale Rd. CH2: Ches 3B 28
Epsom Cl. CH1: Ches 6H 27
Erith M. CH7: Ponty 7C 40
Erith St. CH7: Lees 6C 40
Ermine Rd. CH2: Ches 4A 28 (1E 44)
Erw Fach CH7: M Isa 3K 31
Erw Goed CH7: M Isa 3K 31
Essex Rd. CH2: Ches 3C 28
Estuary Vw. CH5: Ewl 6J 23
Ethelda Dr. CH2: Ches 3C 28
Etna Rd. CH7: Buck 3E 32
Ettrick Pk. CH3: Ches 6C 28
Eurgain Av. CH5: Con Q 2E 22
Evans Easyspace CH5: Dee I 5F 15
Evansleigh Dr. CH5: Sand 5E 24
Evans St. CH6: Flint 7G 7
Eversley Ct. CH2: Ches 4J 27
Eversley Rd. CH2: Ches 4J 27
Ewart St. CH4: Salt F 2B 36
Ewloe Barns Ind. Est. CH7: All 7D 22
Ewloe Castle (remains of) 4F 23
EWLOE GREEN .7F 23
Ewloe Pl. CH7: Buck 2D 32
Exeter Pl. CH1: Ches 3F 27
Expressway Bus. Pk. CH5: Queen 3C 24
Exton Pk. CH1: Ches 5J 27 (1A 44)

F

Facit Glen Ind. Est. CH4: Salt 2F 37
Factory Pool La. CH7: G'field 3D 30
Factory Rd. CH5: Sand 3C 24
Fairfield Rd. CH2: Ches 4C 28
   CH4: Brou 5F 35
   CH5: Queen 3B 24
   CH7: Drury 4H 33
Fairford Rd. CH4: Ches 3F 37
Fairhaven CH8: Holy 4H 5
Fairholme Cl. CH1: Saug 6B 16
Fairoaks Dr. CH5: Con Q 2E 22
Fairview CH4: Penf 3H 41
Fairway CH5: Sand 6E 24
Fairway Cl. CH5: Con Q 3F 23
Fammau Vw. Dr. CH4: Penf 1J 41
Farbailey Cl. CH4: Ches 4H 37
Farfield Av. CH5: Con Q 1G 23
Farfield Rd. CH7: Buck 5D 32
Farm Cl. CH7: Buck 5D 32
Farm Dr. CH5: Con Q 6E 12
Farmfield Cl. CH5: Shot 3K 23
Farm Rd. CH5: Gard C 1C 24
   CH7: Buck 6C 32
Farndon Cl. CH4: Brou 5G 35
Faulkners Cl. CH4: High K 3E 42
Faulkner's La. CH3: Chris 1F 39
Faulkner St. CH2: Ches 5B 28
Feathers La. CH1: Ches 7K 27 (5C 44)
Feathers Lea CH6: Flint 7G 7
          (off Feathers St.)
Feathers St. CH6: Flint 7G 7
Feilden Ct. CH1: Moll 6F 17
Fern Cl. CH6: Flint 2F 11
Fern Ct. CH5: Con Q 7F 13
          (off Church St.)
Ferndale Cl. CH4: Penf 1K 41
Fern Gro. CH5: Ewl 5J 23
Fernhill Rd. CH1: Blac 2E 26
Fernlea Ct. CH1: Saug 7K 15
Fernside Rd. CH5: Aston 4J 23
Ferry Bank CH5: Gard C 2C 24
Ferry Cl. CH5: Sea 2E 24
Ferry Hill CH5: Ewl 6H 23
          (off St David's Cl.)
Ferry La. CH7: Ches 1C 36
Ffordd Aelwyd CH8: Carm 3B 4
Ffordd Argoed CH7: Mold 4H 31
Ffordd Brenig CH7: Bryn B 4A 32
Ffordd Brigog CH7: M Isa 5A 32
Ffordd Bryn Estyn CH7: Mold 5D 30
Ffordd Cae Llwyn CH5: Con Q 3E 22
Ffordd Calcoed CH8: B'ford, Bab 1A 8
Ffordd Celyn CH7: Lees 6C 40
   CH7: S'ton 6H 21
Ffordd Dawel CH7: S'ton 7G 21
Ffordd Derwyn CH4: Penf 3H 41
Ffordd Dol Goed CH7: Mold 6E 30
Ffordd Dwyfor CH8: G'fld 2F 5
Ffordd Edwin CH7: Nor 3G 21

Ffordd Eldon CH7: S'ton 6H 21
Ffordd Estyn CH7: Lees 6C 40
Ffordd Fer CH7: M Isa 4K 31
  CH8: Holy 4F 5
Ffordd Ffynnon CH5: Haw 1H 33
  CH8: Carm 3B 4
Ffordd Ganol CH7: Lea 7H 21
Ffordd Gelfft CH5: Con Q 2E 22
Ffordd Gledlom CH8: Lixm 7B 8
Ffordd Glyn CH7: Mold 6D 30
Ffordd Glyndwr CH6: Flint 2H 11
  CH7: Nor 3G 21
Ffordd Gwelfor CH8: Carm 3B 4
Ffordd Gwynedd CH7: Nor 2G 21
Ffordd Haearn CH4: Penf 2J 41
Ffordd Hengoed CH7: Mold 6E 30
Ffordd Kinderley CH5: Con Q 2F 23
Ffordd Las CH4: Penym 1J 41
  CH7: S'ton 7H 21
Ffordd Llanarth CH5: Con Q 1E 22
Ffordd Llewelyn CH6: Flint 2H 11
Ffordd Meillion CH5: Con Q 3E 22
Ffordd Neuadd CH8: Carm 3B 4
Ffordd Newydd CH5: Con Q 3E 22
  CH7: Mold 6D 30
Ffordd Offa CH7: M Isa 5K 31
Ffordd Ogwen CH7: Bryn B 4A 32
Ffordd Owen CH7: Nor 2G 21
Ffordd Pant Gwyn CH5: Con Q 2E 22
Ffordd Pel-y-Dryn CH5: Haw 1H 33
Ffordd Pennant CH7: Mold 3E 30
Ffordd Pentre CH7: Mold 5G 31
  CH8: Carm 3B 4
Ffordd Siarl CH7: Lees 6C 40
Ffordd Tegid CH5: Ewl 1G 33
Ffordd Tirion CH7: S'ton 7H 21
Ffordd Trem y Foel CH7: Mold 6E 30
Ffordd Walwen CH8: Lixm 7C 8
Ffordd-y-Bont CH7: Ponty, Treu 7A 40
Ffordd y Fran CH6: Flint 3H 11
Ffordd y Glyn CH8: G'fld 2F 5
Ffordd y Graig CH8: Lixm 7C 8
Ffrith Farm La. CH6: Flint 1B 10
Fiddlers La. CH1: Saug 5B 16
Field Cl. CH6: Flint 2F 11
Field Farm La. CH7: Buck 3C 32
Field Farm Rd. CH7: Buck 3C 32
Fielding Cl. CH5: Ewl 1G 33
Field Pk. CH5: Con Q 4E 22
Fieldside CH5: Haw 7A 24
Field Ter. CH6: Bag 4K 5
Field Vw. CH5: Man 5C 24
Fieldway CH1: Saug 5A 16
  CH2: Ches 4A 28
Fifth Av. CH6: Flint 2G 11
Filkin's La. CH3: Ches 7C 28
Finchett Cl. CH1: Ches 5H 27
Finchett Dr. CH1: Ches 5H 27
Firbeck Cl. CH4: Brou 6F 35
Fir Brook Av. CH5: Con Q 1H 23
Firbrook Av. CH5: Haw 6A 24
Firemans Sq. CH1: Ches 3B 44
Fir Gro. CH7: Mold 4E 30
Firs, The CH7: Mold 6G 31
First Av. CH5: Dee I 5D 14
  CH6: Flint 2G 11
Fir Tree Av. CH4: Ches 4H 37
Fir Tree La. CH3: L'ton 7G 29
Fisherman's Rd. CH5: Con Q 7G 13
Fisher Rd. CH1: Blac 4E 26
Five Ashes Rd. CH4: Ches 4G 37
Flag La. Nth. CH2: Upton 7A 18
Flag La. Sth. CH2: Upton 7A 18
Flaxfield Cl. CH8: B'ford 6C 4
Flaxmere Dr. CH3: Gt Bou 1D 38
Fletcher's Bldgs. CH1: Ches 5C 44
Flint Castle (remains of) 7H 7
FLINT COMMUNITY HOSPITAL 1F 11
FLINT MOUNTAIN 6G 11
Flint Rd. CH4: Salt F 7J 25
  CH7: Nor 3H 21
Flintshire Retail Cen. CH6: Flint 7F 7
Flint Station (Rail) 7H 7
FLINT (Y FFLINT) 7G 7
FLOOKERSBROOK 4A 28
Florita Cl. CH5: Con Q 7E 12
Foel Gron CH6: Bag 4C 6
Foregate St. CH1: Ches 7K 27 (4D 44)
Forest Dr. CH4: Brou 6F 35
Forest St. CH1: Ches 7A 28 (4F 44)
Forest Wlk. CH7: Buck 5G 33
Forge Way CH4: Ches 5F 37
Forth Av. CH6: Flint 2G 11
Forum, The CH1: Ches 7J 27 (4B 44)
Forum Shop. Cen. CH1: Ches 7J 27 (4B 44)
Fourth Av. CH5: Dee I 6C 14
Fowler Rd. CH1: Blac 4D 26
Foxcote Cl. CH1: Blac 3D 26
Fox Cover CH3: Guil S 3H 29
Fox Covert La. CH2: Pic 7D 18
  CH2: Upton 5C 18

Foxes Cl. CH5: Man 5C 24
Foxes La. CH7: Buck 3C 32
Foxes Wlk. CH3: Gt Bou 2C 38
Foxes Way CH4: High K 3D 42
Foxglove Cl. CH3: Hunt 3C 38
Fox La. CH3: Wav 4K 39
Fox Lea CH1: Saug 7A 16
Fox's La. CH5: Gard C 2D 24
Foxwist Cl. CH2: Ches 5K 27 (1C 44)
Francis Cl. CH1: Ches 6A 28 (3E 44)
Francis St. CH1: Ches 6A 28 (2E 44)
Fraser Ct. CH4: Ches 2K 37
Fraser Dr. CH7: Buck 5C 32
Friars Ct. CH5: Haw 1A 34
Friars Ga. CH1: Ches 5B 44
Frodsham Ct. CH1: Ches 3C 44
                    (off Frodsham St.)
Frodsham Row CH1: Ches 3C 44
Frodsham Shop. Mall CH1: Ches 3D 44
Frodsham Sq. CH1: Ches 3D 44
Frodsham St. CH1: Ches 6K 27 (3C 44)
Fron Deg CH6: Bag 2B 6
FRON-FAWNOG .5A 30
Fron Heulog CH5: Ewl 7H 23
Fron Pk. Rd. CH8: Holy 4E 4
Fron Rd. CH5: Con Q 2H 23
Fulbrooke CH8: G'fld 1G 5
Furne Rd. CH1: Blac 4E 26

G

GADLYS 5A 6
Gadlys La. CH6: Bag 2K 9
Gainford Av. CH5: Con Q 1F 23
Gala Cl. CH4: Brou 6G 35
Gamul Pl. CH1: Ches 1K 37 (6C 44)
Gamul Ter. CH1: Ches 6C 44
            (off Lwr. Bridge St.)
Gardd Eithin CH7: Nor H 4C 22
Gardd yr Gwanwyn CH7: Nor H 4C 22
GARDEN CITY 1D 24
Garden City Ind. Est. CH5: Gard C 7D 14
Garden Cl. CH1: Ches 6J 27 (3B 44)
Garden La. CH1: Ches 5H 27 (1A 44)
Garden Ter. CH1: Ches 6J 27 (2A 44)
  CH3: Ches 6B 28
Garden Way CH5: Shot 2J 23
Gardner's Row CH6: Flint 3K 11
Garratt Cl. CH5: Con Q 1G 23
Garth Dr. CH2: Ches 3J 27
Garth Ganol CH6: Flint 3H 11
Garthorpe Av. CH5: Con Q 7G 13
Garthorpe Cl. CH5: Con Q 7G 13
Gas La. CH7: Mold 5F 31
Gatesheath Dr. CH2: Upton 1A 28
Gateway Theatre 7J 27 (4B 44)
Gawer Pk. CH1: Ches 4J 27
Gaymoore Cl. CH2: Ches 5J 27 (1A 44)
Gayton Ct. CH2: Ches 3A 28
  CH5: Con Q 2F 23
Gee's Ct. CH3: Ches 7B 28
George Kenyon M. CH4: Salt 3E 36
George St. CH1: Ches 6J 27 (3B 44)
Gerrards Av. CH3: Ches 7C 28
Ger-y-Llan CH7: G'nydd 7B 30
Gladstone Av. CH1: Ches 6H 27
Gladstone Rd. CH1: Ches 5H 27
  CH4: Brou 6F 35
Gladstone St. CH5: Queen 3B 24
  CH5: Shot 2J 23
  CH7: Mold 5F 31
Gladstone Ter. CH5: Pen 5D 24
Gladstone Way CH5: Haw, Queen 1A 34
Glamis Cl. CH3: Ches 6C 28
Glan Aber Cl. CH4: Ches 2G 37
Glan Aber Dr. CH4: Ches 2F 37
Glan Aber Pk. CH4: Ches 2G 37
Glan Alun CH7: Mold 6F 31
Glan Gors CH6: Flint 3H 11
Glan-y-Don CH8: G'fld 3J 5
Glanrafon Rd. CH7: Mold 5F 31
GLANYRAFON 5G 31
Glan yr Eglwys CH7: Nor 2G 21
Glasllwyn Av. CH5: Shot 4K 23
Glastonbury Av. CH2: Upton 1B 28
Glebe Mdws. CH2: Mick T 6H 19
Gleggs Cl. CH3: Gt Bou 2D 38
Glen, The CH1: Blac 2E 26
Glendale Av. CH5: Sand 5D 24
Glendale Bus. Pk. CH5: Sand 5E 24
Gleneagles Cl. CH3: Ches 5D 28
Glenesk Ct. CH5: Gard C 2D 24
Glenside Cl. CH1: Blac 3D 26
Globe Way CH7: Buck 2E 32
Gloucester Av. CH5: Shot 2K 23
Gloucester St. CH1: Ches 5K 27 (1C 44)
Glover's Loom CH3: Gt Bou 2D 38
Gloverstone Ct. CH1: Ches 1K 37 (6C 44)
Glyn Abbott Av. CH8: Holy 4G 5

Glyndwr Ct. CH7: Mold 6G 31
Glyndwr Rd. CH7: G'nydd 7A 30
Glyn Gth. CH1: Blac 5D 26
Glynnedale Pk. CH5: Haw 7J 23
Glynne St. CH5: Con Q 1H 23
  CH5: Queen 3B 24
Glynne Way CH5: Haw 1B 34
Glynteg CH7: Mold 6F 31
Godre'r Coed CH7: G'nydd 7B 30
Godre'r Mynydd CH7: G'nydd 7B 30
Godre'r Waen CH6: Flint M 6G 11
Godstall La. CH1: Ches 4C 44
GOLFTYN 7E 12
Golftyn Dr. CH5: Con Q 6E 12
Golftyn La. CH5: Con Q 6E 12
  CH7: Nor 1C 22
Gonsley Cl. CH2: Ches 5K 27 (1C 44)
Goodwood Cl. CH1: Ches 6H 27
Goodwood Gro. CH7: Lees 5B 40
  CH7: Nor H 4C 22
Gordon La. CH2: Back 2H 17
Gordon Rd. CH1: Blac 4D 26
Gornel Av. CH5: Con Q 1G 23
Gorse Cl. CH4: Penym 1K 41
Gorse Stacks CH1: Ches 6K 27 (3C 44)
Gorse Way CH3: Hunt 4C 38
Gosforth Pl. CH2: Ches 5B 28
Gosmore Rd. CH7: New B 2J 31
Goss St. CH1: Ches 7J 27 (4B 44)
Gowy Rd. CH2: Mick T 6H 19
Goya Cl. CH5: Con Q 7E 12
Grafton St. CH2: Ches 5K 27 (1C 44)
Graham Rd. CH1: Blac 4E 26
Granby Ct. CH5: Con Q 2F 23
Grange Dr. CH2: Ches 4K 27
  CH3: Ches 6E 28
  CH5: Shot 4K 23
  CH8: Holw 4C 4
Grange Rd. W. CH3: Ches 6E 28
Grangeside CH2: Upton 1K 27
Granston Cl. CH5: Con Q 4D 22
Grant Dr. CH5: Ewl 6J 23
Granville Rd. CH1: Ches 5H 27
Grasmere Cl. CH5: Con Q 1E 22
Grasmere Cres. CH7: Buck 3F 33
Grasmere Rd. CH2: Ches 3B 28
Grass Rd. CH7: Ponty 6E 40
Grays Rd. CH7: M Isa 4K 31
GREAT BOUGHTON 2D 38
GREEN, THE 3G 21
Green, The CH4: High K 2E 42
  CH7: Nor 3F 21
  CH8: Lixm 6B 8
Greenacre Dr. CH6: Bag 4D 6
Greenacre Rd. CH4: Ches 5F 37
Greenacres Ct. CH2: Upton 6B 18
Green Bank CH4: Ches 4A 38
Greenbank Dr. CH6: Flint 2E 10
Greenbank La. CH7: S'ton 7J 21
Greenbank Rd. CH7: Ches 4C 28
  CH5: Shot 3J 23
Greenbank Vs. CH6: Flint 1G 11
                    (off Church St.)
Greencroft CH5: Shot 4K 23
                    (off Glasllwyn)
Greenfield Av. CH4: High K 3E 42
Greenfield Bus. Cen. CH8: G'fld 1H 5
Greenfield Bus. Pk. 1 CH8: G'fld 2H 5
Greenfield Bus. Pk. 2 CH8: G'fld 1J 5
  CH3: Wav 3K 39
Greenfield Cres. CH2: Ches 3D 28
GREENFIELD (MAES-GLAS) 2G 5
Greenfield Rd. CH3: Chris, Wav 3K 39
  CH4: Brou 5G 35
  CH8: G'fld 3F 5
Greenfields CH2: Upton 6B 18
Greenfields La. CH3: Row 4H 39
Greenfield St. CH8: Holy 4F 5
Greenfield Valley Heritage Pk. 3G 5
Greenhill Av. CH5: Haw 7J 23
Green La. CH1: Saug 1C 26
  CH2: Pic 6D 18
  CH3: Ches 6E 28
  CH3: Cot E 6K 29
  CH3: Guil S 5E 28
  CH4: Ches 4E 36
  CH4: High K 4E 42
  CH5: Ewl 7E 22
  CH5: Con 1H 06
  CH5: Shot 3K 23
Green La. E. CH5: Sea 5F 15
Green La. Est. CH5: Sea 7G 15
Green La. W. CH5: S'wck 2F 15
Green Mdws. CH5: Haw 1J 33
Green Pk. CH4: Penym 1J 41
  CH5: Con Q 1H 23
Greenside CH7: Mold 5E 30
Greensway CH3: Ches 2G 37
Greenville Av. CH5: Ewl 6G 23
Green Way CH1: Saug 6A 16

Greenway St. CH4: Ches 1K **37** (7C **44**)
Greenwood Av. CH4: Ches 2K **37**
Gresford Av. CH2: Ches 5A **28**
Grey Cl. CH5: Ewl 1G **33**
Grey Friars CH1: Ches 7J **27** (5A **44**)
Greyhound Pk. Rd. CH1: Ches 6F **27**
Greyhound Retail Pk. CH1: Ches 5F **27**
Greystone Rd. CH3: Gt Bou 7E **28**
Griffin Cl. CH1: Blac 2F **27**
Griffiths Ct. CH5: Shot 3J **23**
Griffiths Sq. *CH7: Mold* *4F* ***31***
(off Clayton Rd.)
Grindley Bank CH2: Mick T 7H **19**
Groesffordd CH8: G'fld 1G **5**
Groomscroft CH5: Haw 1K **33**
Groomsdale La. CH5: Haw 1K **33**
Grosvenor Ct. CH1: Ches 7A **28** (4E **44**)
Grosvenor Dr. CH7: Buck 4D **32**
Grosvenor Mus. 1J 37 (6B 44)
GROSVENOR NUFFIELD HOSPITAL 3J 37
Grosvenor Pk. Rd. CH1: Ches 7A **28** (4E **44**)
Grosvenor Pk. Ter. CH1: Ches 7A **28** (5E **44**)
Grosvenor Pl. CH1: Ches 1K **37** (6C **44**)
Grosvenor Rd. CH1: Ches 2J **37** (7A **44**)
CH4: Ches 2J **37** (7A **44**)
CH5: Shot 3K **23**
Grosvenor Shop. Cen. CH1: Ches 7K **27** (5C **44**)
Grosvenor St. CH1: Ches 1J **37** (6B **44**)
CH7: Mold 5F **31**
Grove, The CH7: Nor H 4B **22**
Grove Av. CH3: Ches 5D **28**
Grove Gdns. CH3: L'ton 6G **29**
Grove Rd. CH1: Moll 2D **16**
Groves, The CH1: Ches 1K **37** (6C **44**)
CH5: Shot 1J **23**
Guilden Grn. CH3: Guil S 4G **29**
GUILDEN SUTTON **3H 29**
Guilden Sutton La. CH3: Guil S 4E **28**
(Hare La.)
CH3: Guil S 3F **29**
(Heath Bank)
Guildford Cl. CH4: Ches 3F **37**
Guy La. CH3: Wav 4K **39**
Gwelafon CH8: Holy 4D **4**
Gwel y Mynydd CH7: Buck 4C **32**
Gwenffrwd Rd. CH8: Holy 5E **4**
Gwernaffield Rd. CH7: Mold 3D **30**
GWERNYMYNYDD **7A 30**
Gwylan Av. CH5: Con Q 7G **13**
Gwynedd Dr. CH6: Flint 1G **11**
Gypsy La. CH1: Moll 5F **17**

H

Hadfield Cl. CH5: Con Q 3F **23**
Hadrian Dr. CH1: Blac 2E **26**
Hafan Deg CH7: Mold 6E **30**
CH8: Holw 3D **4**
Hafan Glyd CH5: Shot 2K **23**
Hafod CH6: Flint 1F **11**
Hafod Cl. CH1: Blac 5D **26**
CH5: Con Q 6E **12**
Hafod Dr. CH7: G'nydd 7A **30**
CH8: Pen H 5J **9**
Hafod Pk. CH5: Con Q 6F **13**
CH7: Mold 5D **30**
Hafod Rd. CH7: G'nydd 5A **30**
Hafod-y-Bryn CH8: B'ford 1D **8**
Hafod y Coed CH8: Carm 3A **4**
Hafod-y-Wern CH7: G'nydd 7B **30**
Halkett Cl. CH4: Salt 4E **36**
Halkyn Hall Est. CH8: Pen H 5H **9**
HALKYN (HELYGAIN) **6A 10**
Halkyn Rd. CH2: Ches 5A **28** (1E **44**)
CH6: Flint 4F **11**
CH8: Holy, Milwr 5F **5**
Halkyn St. CH6: Flint 1G **11**
Halkyn Vw. CH5: Con Q 3F **23**
Hallfield Cl. CH6: Flint 1F **11**
Hall La. CH1: S'wck 3F **15**
CH5: Con Q 2G **23**
CH7: S'ton 6G **21**
Hallsgreen La. CH2: Wim T 1H **19**
Hals Cl. CH5: Con Q 7E **12**
Halton Rd. CH2: Upton 2B **28**
Hamilton Av. CH5: Sand 5E **24**
Hamilton Pl. CH1: Ches 7J **27** (4B **44**)
Hamilton Rd. CH5: Con Q 7F **13**
Hamilton St. CH2: Ches 5B **28**
Hampton Av. CH5: Pen 4C **24**
Hampton Rd. CH4: Ches 3F **37**
Hancock's La. CH7: Buck 6C **32**
HANDBRIDGE . . . . . **2K 37 (7D 44)**
Handbridge CH4: Ches 1K **37** (6C **44**)
Handford Rd. CH2: Upton 2A **28**
Hankelow Cl. CH2: Ches 5K **27** (1C **44**)
Hanmer Cl. CH7: Buck 6E **32**
Hanmer Ter. CH6: Bag 2B **6**
Harbour Cl. CH2: Upton 1A **28**
Harding Rd. CH2: Mos 7H **17**
Harebell Cl. CH3: Hunt 3C **38**
Hare La. CH3: Guil S, L'ton 4E **28**
Harington Cl. CH2: Mos 6J **17**
Harington Rd. CH2: Mos 7J **17**
Harlech Av. CH5: Con Q 1F **23**
Harlech Cl. CH7: Buck 2E **32**
Harrison Gro. CH5: Sand 5E **24**
Harrowby Rd. CH7: Mold 4F **31**
Hartford M. *CH3: Ches* *7D* ***28***
(off Pearl La.)
Hartford Way CH1: Ches 7F **27**
Harthill Rd. CH1: Blac 2E **26**
Hartington St. CH4: Ches 2K **37** (7D **44**)
Hartley Cl. CH4: High K 3D **42**
Haslin Cres. CH3: Chris 2F **39**
Hassalls La. CH2: Bri T 4H **19**
Hatchmere Dr. CH3: Gt Bou 1D **38**
Hatherton Way CH2: Ches 5K **27** (1C **44**)
Hatton Rd. CH1: Blac 3E **26**
Haulfryn CH7: S'ton 7G **21**
HAWARDEN AIRPORT **2H 35**
Hawarden Bridge Station (Rail) **7A 14**
Hawarden Castle 2C 34
Hawarden Dr. CH7: Drury 4H **33**
Hawarden High School Sports Cen. 7J 23
Hawarden Ind. Pk. CH5: Haw 3F **35**
Hawarden Old Castle 2B 34
HAWARDEN (PENARLAG) **1B 34**
Hawarden Rd. CH4: Penf 2J **41**
Hawarden Station (Rail) **1A 34**
Hawarden Way CH5: Man 6C **24**
Hawker Cl. CH4: Brou 5G **35**
Hawkesbury Rd. CH7: Buck 4D **32**
Hawklane Cl. CH5: Con Q 2E **22**
Hawthorn Av. CH7: Mold 4E **30**
Hawthorn Cl. CH5: Aston 5K **23**
Hawthorne Av. CH5: Con Q 1F **23**
CH7: Buck 5E **32**
Hawthorne Vw. CH5: Gard C 1E **24**
Hawthorn Rd. CH3: Chris 2G **39**
CH4: Ches 4F **37**
Haydock Cl. CH1: Ches 6H **27**
CH7: Lees 5B **40**
Haydon Ct. CH2: Ches 4K **27**
Haydon Way CH5: Gard C 2D **24**
Hayes Pk. CH1: Ches 5J **27**
Haygarth Hgts. CH1: Ches 3E **44**
Haymakers Cl. CH4: Ches 5F **37**
Haymakers Way CH1: Saug 7A **16**
Hazel Ct. CH6: Flint 2E **10**
Hazel Dr. CH4: Penf 1K **41**
Hazel Gro. CH7: Mold 4E **30**
Hazel Rd. CH4: Ches 4F **37**
Hazelwood Cl. CH5: Con Q 3F **23**
Hazelwood Cres. CH5: Haw 2H **33**
Headlands, The CH3: Ches 4E **44**
Health St. CH5: Shot 2K **23**
Heath Bank CH3: Guil S 3F **29**
Heath Cl. CH3: Gt Bou 1D **38**
Heathcote Cl. CH2: Ches 5J **27**
Heather Ct. CH3: Gt Bou 1C **38**
Heathfields Cl. CH2: Ches 5K **27**
Heath La. CH2: Lit S 1K **17**
CH2: Stoak 1B **18**
CH3: Ches, Gt Bou 1C **38**
Heath Rd. CH2: Upton 1K **27**
Heath Ter. CH2: Upton 7A **18**
Hedgerow, The CH5: Haw 7H **23**
Heinzel Pk. CH6: Flint 7F **7**
Helsby By-Pass CH1: Moll 3B **16**
Henblas CH6: Flint M 6G **11**
CH7: Mold 5E **30**
Hendir CH6: Flint M 6G **11**
Hendy Rd. CH7: G'nydd, Mold 5C **30**
Henffordd CH7: Mold 4F **31**
Hen Fuarth CH8: Holy 5F **5**
Henley Av. CH5: Con Q 2H **23**
Henley Rd. CH4: Ches 3F **37**
Henrietta St. CH5: Shot 2K **23**
Henry Pl. CH1: Ches 6K **27** (2C **44**)
Henry Taylor St. CH6: Flint 7H **7**
Henry Wood Ct. CH4: Salt 3E **36**
Henshall St. CH1: Ches 5J **27** (1A **44**)
Heol Fammau CH7: M Isa 3K **31**
Heol Tywysog CH8: Pen H 5J **9**
Heol-y-Brenin CH8: Holy 4F **5**
Heol-y-Bryn CH6: Flint 3H **11**
Heol-y-Dderwen CH7: Lees 6B **40**
Heol y Gordon CH7: Lees 6B **40**
Heol-y-Wern CH7: G'nydd 7B **30**
Hereford Pl. CH1: Blac 3G **27**
Hereward Rd. CH3: Ches 7D **28**
Heritage Ct. CH1: Ches 7K **27** (6C **44**)
CH7: Mold *4F* ***31***
(off Clayton Rd.)
Hermitage Ct. CH1: Saug 7A **16**
Hermitage Rd. CH1: Saug 7A **16**
Heron Cl. CH4: Brou 5G **35**
Heron Pl. CH2: Ches 5K **27** (1C **44**)
Herons Way CH4: Ches 6H **37**
Herriot Gro. CH5: Ewl 1G **33**
Hewitt's La. CH7: Buck 5C **32**
Hewitt St. CH2: Ches 5B **28**
Hexham Ct. *CH1: Ches* *6H* ***27***
Heywoods, The CH2: Ches 4J **27**
Hickmore Heys CH3: Guil S 4H **29**
Highcliffe Av. CH1: Ches 4H **27**
Highcroft CH5: Shot 3J **23**
Highcroft, The CH5: Con Q 2E **22**
Higher Cl. CH5: Con Q 1E **22**
Higher Comn. Cl. CH7: Buck 3E **32**
Higher Comn. Rd. CH7: Buck 3E **32**
Higher Comn. Way CH7: Buck 3E **32**
Higher Ferry La. CH1: Ches 1B **36**
HIGHER KINNERTON **3E 42**
HIGHER SHOTTON **3J 23**
Higher Shotton Farm CH5: Shot 3J **23**
Highfield CH5: Haw 1A **34**
CH6: Bag 3B **6**
Highfield Av. CH7: M Isa 4A **32**
Highfield Dr. CH7: Buck 6E **32**
Highfield Rd. CH1: Blac 3D **26**
Highfields CH4: Penf 5K **41**
Highfield Vs. CH7: Mold 6F **31**
Highland Av. CH5: Aston 4J **23**
High Mdw. Ct. CH6: Flint 1F **11**
Highmere Dr. CH5: Con Q 1E **22**
High Pk. CH5: Haw 7A **24**
High St. CH4: Salt 3D **36**
CH5: Con Q 7G **13**
CH6: Bag, Flint 2A **6**
CH7: Mold 4F **31**
CH7: Nor 3G **21**
CH8: Holy 5F **5**
Highvale CH5: Con Q 1E **22**
Highway, The CH5: Ewl, Haw 7J **23**
Hilary Cl. CH3: Gt Bou 7D **28**
Hilbre Rd. CH5: Con Q 7F **13**
Hillary Gro. CH7: Buck 5D **32**
Hillcourt Av. CH6: Bag 5D **6**
Hillfield Rd. CH5: Aston 5K **23**
Hilliards Ct. CH4: Ches 6H **37**
Hill Rd. CH4: Ecc 7A **38**
Hillsdown Dr. CH5: Con Q 2E **22**
Hillside CH5: Haw 7A **24**
Hillside Av. CH5: Con Q 1F **23**
Hillside Ct. CH8: Holy 4F **5**
Hillside Cres. CH7: Buck 6D **32**
CH7: Mold 3E **30**
Hillside Rd. CH1: Blac 4E **26**
CH4: Penf 1J **41**
Hillside Way CH6: Flint 2F **11**
Hills Lea *CH6: Flint* *7G* ***7***
(off Coleshill St.)
Hillsview Rd. CH7: Buck 5D **32**
Hilltop Cl. CH5: Ewl 6G **23**
Hilltop Rd. CH3: Guil S 3H **29**
Hill Vw. CH7: Bryn B 3K **31**
Hobart Way CH1: Blac 4D **26**
Hob La. CH2: Wim T 1J **19**
WA6: Dun H 1J **19**
Holbein Cl. CH4: Ches 3K **37**
Holkham, The CH3: Ches 7D **28**
Hollies, The CH7: Buck 3E **32**
Hollins La. CH5: Haw 2H **33**
Hollowbrook Dr. CH5: Con Q 2E **22**
Holly Cl. CH2: Mick T 7H **19**
CH5: Con Q 6E **12**
CH7: Buck 4D **32**
Holly Ct. *CH5: Con Q* *7F* ***13***
(off Church St.)
CH7: Lees 5B **40**
Holly Dr. CH4: Penf 1K **41**
CH7: Mold 4E **30**
Holly Grange CH5: Con Q 1F **23**
Holly Gro. CH5: Aston 5K **23**
Holly Rd. CH4: Ches 4F **37**
HOLWAY **3C 4**
Holway Ct. CH8: Holw 3C **4**
Holway Rd. CH8: Holw, Holy 3C **4**
Holyrood Way CH3: Ches 5D **28**
Holy Tree Cl. CH5: Ewl 7G **23**
Holywell Leisure Cen. 5F 5
Holywell Rd. CH5: Ewl 5F **23**
CH6: Bag 4J **5**
CH6: Flint 7G **7**
CH7: Nor 2F **2**
Holywell St. CH6: Flint 7G **7**
HOLYWELL (TREFFYNNON) **5F 5**
Home Cl. CH3: Chris 2G **39**
Homedee Ho. CH1: Ches 2B **4**
Home Pk. CH1: Moll 6F **1**
Honeysuckle Cl. CH4: Brou 6G **3**
HONKLEY **7G 4**
HOOLE **5B 2**
HOOLE BANK **1E 2**
Hoole Bri. CH1: Ches 5A **28** (1E **44**
CH2: Ches 5A **28** (1E **44**
Hoole Gdns. CH2: Ches 5D **2**
Hoole Ho. CH2: Ches 4D **2**
Hoole La. CH2: Ches 6B **2**
Hoole Pk. CH2: Ches 5B **2**

Hoole Rd. CH2: Ches 5A 28
HOOLE VILLAGE 2E 28
Hoole Way CH1: Ches 6K 27 (2D 44)
Hope Rd. CH4: Brou 6F 35
Hope St. CH4: Salt 3F 37
Hope Vw. CH4: Penf 3J 41
Hopkinson Ct. CH1: Ches 7H 27 (4A 44)
Hornbeam Av. CH7: Buck 5G 33
Hornbeam Cl. CH2: Ches 5D 28
Hornesby Cl. CH5: Con Q 7E 12
Horrocks Rd. CH2: Upton 3A 28
HOSPICE OF THE GOOD SHEPHERD 3H 17
Hough Grn. CH4: Ches 2G 37
Houghton Cl. CH2: Ches 6B 28
Housesteads Dr. CH2: Ches 5B 28
Housman Cl. CH1: Blac 3G 27
Howard Rd. CH4: Salt 3D 36
Howards Cl. CH4: Penf 2J 41
Howard St. CH5: Con Q 1H 23
Howe Rd. CH4: Ches 2H 37
Hugh St. CH4: Ches 2K 37
Hulleys Cl. CH4: Penym 1K 41
Hunters Cft. CH4: High K 3D 42
Hunter St. CH1: Ches 6J 27 (4B 44)
Hunter's Wlk. CH1: Ches 7J 27 (4B 44)
HUNTINGTON 3C 38
Hunts Cl. CH3: Gt Bou 7D 28
Hurlbutts Dr. CH5: Queen 3A 24
Hurlestone Cl. CH2: Mick T 6H 19
Hurstwood CH3: Wav 5J 39
Huxleys La. LL12: Hope 7K 41

I

Imperial Av. CH1: Blac 4C 26
Ince La. CH2: Wim T 1H 19
Ingham Cl. CH3: Ches 7C 28
Institute La. CH7: Nor H 4C 22
Irving's Cres. CH4: Salt 3E 36
Isabella Ct. CH4: Salt 3E 36
CH5: Con Q 1G 23
Isglan Rd. CH8: Whit 2B 4
Issa Farm Courtyard CH7: Bryn B 3A 32
Iver Cl. CH2: Upton 1A 28
Iver Rd. CH2: Upton 1A 28
Ivy Ct. CH5: Con Q 7F 13
(off Church St.)
Ivy Cres. CH7: Mold 4E 30
Ivy M. CH2: Ches 3C 28

J

Jackson Ct. CH5: Haw 2F 35
James Pl. CH2: Ches 6B 28
James St. CH1: Ches 6K 27 (2D 44)
Jamieson Cl. CH3: Ches 6C 28
Jasmine Cres. CH7: Mold 4E 30
Jefferson Rd. CH5: Ewl 6J 23
Jesmond Rd. CH1: Ches 6H 27
Johnsons Cl. CH4: Ches 4H 37
Johnson's Ct. CH4: Ches 1K 37 (7C 44)
Jonathan's Way CH1: Blac 3E 26
Jubilee Ct. CH7: Buck 5E 32
Jubilee Dr. CH8: Halk 6A 10
Jubilee Rd. CH7: Buck 5E 32
Jubilee St. CH5: Shot 2K 23
Julius Cl. CH6: Flint 2J 11
Juniper Cl. CH5: Con Q 1F 23
Juniper Ct. CH2: Ches 4D 28
Jupiter Dr. CH1: Ches 6E 26

K

Kaleyards CH1: Ches 6K 27 (3C 44)
Kearsley Av. CH5: Haw 7J 23
Keats Cl. CH5: Ewl 1H 33
Keats Ter. CH1: Blac 3G 27
KELSTERTON 5D 12
Kelsterton Ct. CH5: Con Q 6E 12
Kelsterton La. CH6: Kel 2B 22
CH7: Kel, Nor 2B 22
Kelsterton Rd. CH5: Con Q 4C 12
CH6: Kel, Con Q 5D 12
Kelvin Gro. CH2: Ches 4A 28
Kempert Cl. CH1: Ches 6H 27
Kendal Cl. CH2: Ches 2C 28
Kenilworth Av. CH1: Ches 6C 44
Kennedy Cl. CH2: Ches 3C 28
Kennedy Dr. CH5: Haw 6B 24
Kennington Cres. CH5: Queen 4B 24
Kensington Av. CH5: Shot 3J 23
Kensington Grn. CH3: Ches 3F 37
Kensington Rd. CH4: Ches 3G 37
Kenstone Cl. CH7: Mold 5G 31
Kent Av. CH5: Shot 3K 23
Kent Cl. CH4: Penym 1K 41
Kent Ho. CH2: Ches 3B 28

Kent Rd. CH2: Ches 3B 28
CH5: Con Q 7F 13
Keristal Av. CH3: Gt Bou 2C 38
Kestrel Cl. CH5: Con Q 3F 23
Keswick Cl. CH2: Ches 3C 28
Ketlan Ct. CH4: Salt 2E 36
Ketland Cl. CH5: Shot 2A 24
Ketland Pl. CH5: Shot 2K 23
Killins La. CH5: Shot 3J 23
Kilmorey Pk. CH2: Ches 4B 28
Kilmorey Pk. Av. CH2: Ches 5A 28
Kilmorey Pk. Rd. CH2: Ches 5B 28
Kiln Cl. CH6: Flint 1G 11
CH7: Buck 4C 32
Kimberley Ter. CH2: Ches 6B 28
CH6: Bag 4K 5
(off New Brighton Rd.)
King Charles Ct. CH1: Ches 3B 44
CH2: Ches 2B 44
(off Victoria Rd.)
King Charles Tower 3C 44
King Edward Dr. CH6: Flint 2G 11
King Edward St. CH5: Shot 2K 23
Kingfisher Ct. CH2: Ches 5J 27 (1B 44)
King George St. CH5: Shot 3J 23
Kings Av. CH6: Flint 2H 11
CH8: G'fld 2G 5
Kings Bldgs. CH1: Ches 6J 27 (3B 44)
Kingsbury Cl. CH6: Flint 1E 10
Kings Cl. CH4: Ches 4F 37
Kings Ct. CH1: Ches 6J 27 (3B 44)
Kings Cres. E. CH3: Ches 7C 28
Kings Cres. W. CH3: Ches 7C 28
King's Cft. CH5: Con Q 6F 13
(off King's Rd.)
Kingsfield Ct. CH1: Ches 6J 37
Kingsley Gdns. CH3: Gt Bou 1D 38
Kingsley Rd. CH3: Ches 1D 38
CH5: Gard C 1D 24
Kingsmead CH2: Upton 1J 27
KINGS MEADOWS 6H 37
King's Rd. CH5: Con Q 7F 13
Kingston Ct. CH5: Saug 5B 16
Kingston Dr. CH5: Con Q 1F 23
King St. CH1: Ches 6J 27 (3B 44)
CH7: Lees 5B 40
CH7: Mold 4F 31
Kingsway CH2: Ches 4B 28
CH5: Shot 2J 23
Kingsway W. CH2: Ches 4A 28
Kingswood Av. CH1: Saug 6C 16
Kingswood La. CH1: Saug 6C 16
Kinnerton Cl. CH4: Salt 4D 36
KINNERTON GREEN 3F 43
Kinnerton Hgts. CH4: High K 3E 42
Kinnerton La. CH4: High K 1B 42
Kinnerton Old Rd. CH4: Brou 5A 34
CH5: Dob 5A 34
Kinnerton Rd. CH4: D'ton, Low K 1H 43
CH4: High K 7A 42
LL12: Hope 7A 42
Kipling Cl. CH5: Ewl 1G 33
Kipling Rd. CH1: Blac 3F 27
Kirby Cl. CH2: Ches 3K 27
Kirkett Av. CH4: High K 3D 42
Kirkwood Cl. CH3: Ches 6C 28
Kitchen St. CH1: Ches 7H 27 (4A 44)
Knightsbridge Ct. CH1: Ches 7A 28 (5E 44)
Knights Grn. CH6: Flint 1G 11
Knowle La. CH7: Buck 4E 32
Knowsley Ct. CH2: Ches 4B 28
Knowsley Rd. CH2: Ches 4B 28
Knutsford Way CH1: Ches 6F 27
Kohima Cres. CH3: Hunt 4D 38
Kus Ind. Est. CH5: Haw 3E 34
Kynaston Dr. CH4: Salt F 2C 36

L

Laburnum Gro. CH4: Salt 3E 36
LACHE 4F 37
Lache Hall Cres. CH4: Ches 5F 37
Lache La. CH4: Bald 7D 36
CH4: Marl L, Ches 7D 36
Lache Pk. Av. CH4: Ches 3G 37
Lakeside CH4: Ches 7H 37
(not continuous)
Lakeside Bus. Village CH5: Ewl 7G 23
CH7: Buck 2D 32
Lakewood Ct. CH7: Buck 7H 37
Lambs La. CH7: Buck 5F 33
Lancaster Dr. CH5: Ewl 6D 28
Lancaster Pk. CH3: Brou 6E 34
Langdale Av. CH1: Ches 4F 33
Langdon Ho. CH4: Ches 2H 37
(off Hough Grn.)
Langford Cres. CH7: Buck 5B 32
Langport Dr. CH3: Ches 6E 28
Lansdowne Gro. CH4: Ches 2G 37

Lansdowne Dr. CH5: Con Q 6F 13
Lansdown Rd. CH4: Brou 6F 35
Larch Av. CH5: Shot 4K 23
Larches, The CH5: Haw 2H 33
Larchfields CH1: Saug 7A 16
Larch Way CH4: Salt 3E 36
Larksfield Cl. LL12: Hope 7K 41
Larkspur Cl. CH4: Ches 5F 37
Larne Dr. CH4: Brou 5H 35
Laurel Dr. CH7: Buck 5E 32
Laurel Gro. CH7: Buck 5C 28
Lavender Ct. CH5: Shot 2K 23
Lawn Dr. CH2: Upton 1K 27
Lawn-y-Pentre CH6: Flint M 6G 11
Lawrence St. CH5: Sand 5E 24
Laws Gdns. CH3: Gt Bou 1C 38
Law St. CH2: Ches 5B 28
LEA BY BACKFORD 4G 17
Leaches Cl. CH5: Man 5C 24
Leaches La. CH5: Man 7C 24
(not continuous)
Leadbrook Dr. CH6: Flint 3K 11
LEADMILL 4G 31
Lead Mills CH7: Mold 4G 31
Lea Dr. CH7: Buck 5E 32
Leadworks La. CH1: Ches 6A 28 (3E 44)
Lea Hall Pk. CH1: Lea B 4G 17
Leahurst Cl. CH2: Ches 4B 28
Leaside Rd. CH1: Blac 2E 26
Ledsham La. CH5: Haw 3J 33
Leen La. CH1: Ches 4C 44
Lee St. CH1: Ches 6A 28
LEESWOOD (COED-LLAI) 6C 40
Leeswood Rd. CH7: Buck 5D 32
Leighstone Ct. CH2: Ches 5J 27 (1B 44)
Leighton Ct. CH5: Con Q 7G 13
Leonard St. CH1: Ches 5H 27
Lester La. CH4: Brou, High K 6D 34
Lesters La. CH4: Low K 6J 35
Level Rd. CH5: Haw 2H 33
Lexham Grn. Cl. CH7: Buck 5E 32
Leyfield Ct. CH4: Ches 4F 37
Leyland Dr. CH4: Salt F 3B 36
Lichfield Rd. CH1: Blac 3F 27
Lightfoot St. CH2: Ches 5A 28
Lilac Dr. CH4: Penf 2J 41
Lily Ter. CH8: B'ford 7D 4
Lime Cl. CH5: Con Q 1E 22
Lime Gro. CH2: Ches 5B 28
CH4: Salt 3D 36
Lincoln Dr. CH2: Ches 3C 28
Lincoln Rd. CH1: Blac 3F 27
CH5: Ewl 6J 23
Lindale Cl. CH5: Con Q 1E 22
Linden Av. CH5: Con Q 7F 13
Linden Cl. CH5: Con Q 7F 13
Linden Dr. CH2: Mick T 6H 19
CH7: Mold 6D 30
Linden Gro. CH2: Ches 3D 36
CH4: Salt 3D 36
Linderick Av. CH7: Buck 3C 32
Lindfields CH4: Ches 3E 36
Lindum Cl. CH7: New B 2J 31
Linen Hall Pl. CH1: Ches 7J 27 (4A 44)
Linksway CH2: Upton 1J 27
Linthorpe Cl. CH4: Ches 4E 32
Linthorpe Gdns. CH7: Buck 5E 32
Linthorpe Rd. CH7: Buck 4D 32
Linwood Cl. CH4: Penf 1K 41
Lit. Abbey Gateway CH1: Ches 6K 27 (3B 44)
LITTLE HEATH 7G 29
Little Heath CH3: Chris 1G 39
Lit. Heath Rd. CH3: Chris, L'ton 7G 29
LITTLE MANCOT 6C 24
Little Mere CH3: Chris 1G 39
LITTLE MOUNTAIN 6H 33
Lit. Mountain Ind. Pk. CH7: Buck 5G 33
Lit. Mountain Rd. CH7: Buck 6H 33
Little Roodee CH5: Haw 2F 35
Lit. St John St. CH1: Ches 7K 27 (5D 44)
LITTLETON 6G 29
Littleton La. CH3: L'ton 6G 29
Liverpool Rd. CH2: Back, Mos 3H 17
CH2: Mos, Ches, Upton 5J 27 (1B 44)
CH5: Ewl 3D 32
(Mold Rd.)
CH5: Ewl 6H 23
(Old Aston Hill)
CH7: Buck 3D 32
LIXWM (LLGSWM) 7C 8
Lixwm Rd. CH8: B'ford 3C 8
Llandore Cl. CH5: Con Q 4E 22
Llanfair Cres. CH5: Con Q 4E 22
Lleprog La. CH6: Flint 7A 6
Llewellyn Dr. CH7: Bryn B 3A 32
Llewellyn St. CH5: Shot 3A 32
Lllys-y-Wern CH7: S'ton 7G 21
LLONG 7A 32
Llon yr Orsaf CH7: Mold 5G 31
Lloyd Pl. CH1: Blac 4E 26
Lloyds Hill CH7: Drury 3G 33

Lloyd St. CH6: Flint 7H 7
Llwyn Aled CH8: Holy 5E 4
Llwyn Bach CH7: Mold 6D 30
Llwyn Beuno CH8: Holy 4E 4
(off New Rd.)
Llwyn Derw CH7: M Isa 3K 31
Llwyn Eithin CH7: Mold 6E 30
Llwyni Dr. CH5: Con Q 3E 22
LLWYN-IFOR .1B 4
Llwyn-Ifor La. CH8: Whit 1B 4
Llwynon Cl. CH7: Bryn B 4A 32
Llwyn Onn CH6: Flint 5H 11
Llwyn Onn La. CH7: Nor 5H 11
Llyns Alyn CH5: Con Q 3E 22
Llys Ambrose CH7: Mold 6D 30
Llys Ann CH7: Lees 6C 40
Llys Argoed CH7: M Isa 5J 31
Llys Armon CH7: Lixm 7B 8
Llys Ben CH7: Nor H 4C 22
Llys Berllan CH7: Buck 4B 32
Llys Brenig CH5: Ewl 1G 33
Llys Bryn Eglwys CH7: Mold 4F 31
Llys Caer CH4: Brou 6E 34
Llys Cae'r Glo CH7: S'ton 7G 21
Llys Daniel Owen CH7: Mold 3E 30
Llys Dedwydd CH7: M Isa 4K 31
CH8: Pen H 4H 9
Llys Derwen CH4: High K 2D 42
CH7: Mold 5G 31
Llys Eglwys CH8: G'fld 2G 5
Llys Eithin CH7: Nor H 4C 22
Llys Enfys CH7: G'nydd 7A 30
CH7: Rhos 2A 20
Llys Fammau CH7: M Isa 4K 31
Llys Gwynant CH7: Bryn B 3A 32
Llys John Dafis CH7: Mold 3F 31
Llys Mai CH7: Buck 4D 32
Llys Menden CH7: Mold 5D 30
Llys Mervyn CH7: Mold 3E 30
Llys Nercwys CH7: Mold 6G 31
Llys Padarn CH5: Ewl 1G 33
Llys Pant Derw CH5: Con Q 2E 22
Llys Pen-y-Glyn CH6: Flint M 6F 11
Llys Plas Newydd CH4: High K 4F 43
Llys Pont Garreg CH7: Mold 6F 31
Llys Pont-y-Felin CH7: Mold 3F 31
Llys Preswylfa CH7: Mold 5E 30
Llys Saron CH8: B'ford 7D 4
Llys Tudela CH7: Mold 5D 30
Llys Wylfa CH7: M Isa 4K 31
Llys-y-Berllan CH8: G'fld 2F 5
Llys y Brenin CH8: Holy 5F 5
(off Park La.)
Llys y Coed CH7: Mold 7G 31
Llys y Foel CH7: Mold 6G 31
Llys y Fron CH8: Holy 5F 5
Llys-y-Fron CH7: Mold 5D 30
Llys y Maesteg CH8: G'fld 3J 5
Llys-y-Mor CH8: Carm 3B 4
Llys y Nant CH7: Buck 6D 32
Llys-y-Nant CH7: Mold 6G 31
CH8: Pen H 5J 9
Llys yr Awel CH7: Mold 6G 31
Llys yr Efail CH7: Mold 5F 31
Llys y Wennol CH7: Nor H 4C 22
Lockside Ct. CH3: Ches 6B 28
(off Hoole La.)
Lodge Gdns. CH2: Upton 2K 27
Lodge La. CH1: Saug 3J 15
Lon Cae Del CH5: Ewl 1H 33
CH7: Mold 5D 30
Lon Celyn CH5: Con Q 1F 23
Lon Oderwen CH5: Con Q 1F 23
London Rd. CH7: S'ton 7G 21
Longacre Dr. CH6: Bag 4C 6
Longburgh Cl. CH2: Ches 5B 28
Longdale Dr. CH2: Ches 3C 26
Longfellow Av. CH5: Ewl 1G 33
Longfield Av. CH2: Upton 1A 28
Long La. CH1: Saug 5B 16
CH2: Ches, Upton 7A 18
CH3: Wav 7A 18
Lon Goed CH8: Holw 3C 4
Lon Groes CH6: Flint 1F 11
Lon Gwynant CH5: Ewl 1G 33
Lon Isaf CH7: Mold 5G 31
Lon Llwyni CH5: Con Q 3E 22
Lonsdale Ct. CH4: Ches 5F 37
Lon-y-Berth CH7: Mold 6D 30
Lon-y-Fron CH8: Pen H 5J 9
Lon-y-Gog CH7: Nor 6H 11
Lon y Mynydd CH8: B'ford 6B 4
Lon y Parc CH7: Mold 6E 30
Lon y Plas CH6: Flint M 5F 11
Lord St. CH3: Ches 6B 28
Lorne St. CH1: Ches 6J 27 (2A 44)
Louise St. CH1: Ches 6J 27 (2A 44)
Love La. CH7: Mold 4F 31
Love St. CH1: Ches 7K 27 (4D 44)
Lwr. Aston Hall La. CH5: Aston 5K 23
Lwr. Bridge St. CH1: Ches 7K 27 (5C 44)

Lwr. Brook St. CH5: Con Q 6F 13
Lwr. Dee Vw. Rd. CH8: G'fld 2G 5
Lower Fld. Rd. CH4: Ches 4G 37
LOWER KINNERTON 1H 43
Lwr. Mountain Rd. CH4: Hope, Penf 4K 41
LL12: Hope 4K 41
Lwr. Mumforth St. CH6: Flint 7H 7
Lwr. Park Rd. CH4: Ches 7A 28 (6E 44)
Lwr. Sydney St. CH5: Flint 7H 7
Lucerne Cl. CH3: Hunt 3D 38
Ludlow Rd. CH1: Blac 3G 27
Ludwell Cl. CH4: Ches 3H 37
Lumley Cl. CH1: Ches 7K 27 (5D 44)
Lumley Rd. CH2: Ches 4J 27
Lupin Dr. CH3: Hunt 3D 38
Lyme Gro. CH7: Buck 5F 33
Lynfield Cl. CH5: Con Q 1F 23
Lynton Cl. CH4: Ches 3F 37
Lynton Pl. CH4: Brou 5F 35
Lynwood Rd. CH1: Blac 3F 27
Lyon St. CH1: Ches 6K 27 (2D 44)
Lyons Yd. CH5: Pen 4C 24

M

Machynlleth Way CH5: Con Q 2E 22
McKeown Cl. CH5: Con Q 3E 22
Madeley Cl. CH4: Brou 5G 35
Maelor Cl. CH7: Buck 6E 32
Maengwyn Av. CH5: Con Q 1E 22
Maes Afon CH6: Flint 2F 11
Maes Alaw CH6: Flint 2H 11
Maes Bodlonfa CH7: Mold 5E 30
Maes Celyn CH7: Nor 2F 21
Maes Cynfaen CH8: B'ford 7C 4
Maes Glanrafon CH7: Mold 5F 31
(off Brook St.)
Maes Glas CH5: Ewl 1H 33
CH6: Flint 1F 11
Maes Gruffydd CH7: S'ton 7G 21
MAES GRUFFYDD 7F 21
Maes Gwalia CH7: S'ton 7H 21
Maes Gwelfor CH8: Pen H 4H 9
Maes Gwern CH7: Mold 7E 30
Maes Gwyn CH6: Flint 2H 11
Maes Hyfryd CH6: Flint 2G 11
Maes Lygan CH8: Pen H 5H 9
Maes Owen CH7: Mold 3E 30
Maes Teg CH6: Flint 3G 11
Maes Uchaf CH5: Con Q 4E 22
Maes Welwen CH6: Bag 3J 5
Maes Wepre CH5: Con Q 3E 22
Maes-y-Coed CH4: Salt 3E 36
CH6: Flint 2F 11
MAES-Y-DRE .3E 30
Maes y Dre CH7: Mold 4F 31
Maes-y-Dre Av. CH6: Flint 2H 11
Maes-y-Dyffryn CH8: G'fld 2G 5
Maes y March CH7: Mold 4E 30
Maes y Meillion CH7: Lees 6B 40
Maes y Plwm CH8: Holw 3C 4
Maes-yr-Afon CH8: Holy 4H 5
Maes yr Haf CH7: Mold 5E 30
Maes yr Haul CH7: Mold 6E 30
Maes yr Odyn CH8: Holy 5G 5
Maes yr Ysgol CH6: Flint 1F 11
Magazine La. CH5: Ewl 6D 22
Main Rd. CH4: Brou 5F 35
CH4: High K, Low K 3D 42
CH7: New B, S'ton 2G 31
Mainwaring Dr. CH4: Salt F 2C 36
Maitland Way CH1: Blac 4D 26
Makepeace Cl. CH3: Ches 5E 28
Mallory Wlk. CH4: D'ton 6J 43
Mallow Cl. CH3: Hunt 3C 38
Malta Rd. CH2: Mos 6H 17
Malvern Rd. CH1: Blac 3G 27
Manbry Cl. CH5: Con Q 1E 22
Mancot La. CH5: Man, Pen 5B 24
MANCOT ROYAL 5C 24
Mancot Royal Cl. CH5: Man 5B 24
Mancot Way CH5: Man 5C 24
Manley Ct. CH5: Shot 1K 23
Mannings La. CH2: Hoole V 2D 28
Mannings La. Sth. CH2: Ches 3C 28
Manor Cres. CH5: Haw 1G 35
Manor Dr. CH3: Gt Bou 7D 28
CH6: Flint 5D 6
CH7: Buck 5E 32
Manor Farm Cl. CH2: Mick T 7H 19
Manor Farm Ct. CH5: Haw 2F 35
Manor Ind. Est. CH6: Flint 4D 6
Manor La. CH5: Haw 3E 34
Manor La. Ind. Est. CH5: Haw 2F 35
Manor Pk. CH7: S'ton 7G 21
Manor Rd. CH4: Ches 4H 37
CH5: Sea 2E 24
Mansfield Av. CH5: Haw 1H 33
Maple Cres. CH5: Haw 2H 33

Maple Gro. CH2: Ches 4D 28
CH4: Salt 4D 36
Maplewood Av. CH5: Gard C 1D 24
Maplewood Gro. CH1: Saug 7B 16
Marbury Av. CH7: Buck 6E 32
Marbury Rd. CH3: Ches 6E 28
Mare Hey La. CH5: Ewl 7G 23
(Holy Tree Cl.)
CH5: Ewl 7H 23
(St Davids Pk.)
Marian Cl. CH6: Flint 3H 11
Marian Dr. CH3: Gt Bou 1D 38
Marina Dr. CH2: Upton 1A 28
CH5: Shot 2K 23
Mark Cl. CH2: Ches 6B 28
Market Sq. CH1: Ches 4B 44
CH6: Flint 7G 7
Market Way CH1: Ches 4B 44
Marlborough Av. CH5: Haw 1H 33
Marlborough Ct. CH3: Ches 6D 28
Marl Cft. CH3: Gt Bou 2D 38
Marley Way CH4: Salt 2E 36
Marl Heys CH2: Upton 1A 28
Marlow Av. CH2: Upton 2B 28
Marlowe Av. CH5: Con Q 2H 23
Marlowe Cl. CH1: Blac 3G 27
Marlow Ter. CH7: Mold 5F 31
Marlston Av. CH4: Ches 3G 37
Marlwood Pl. CH4: Brou 6E 34
Marnel Dr. CH5: Pen 4C 24
Marsh La. CH6: Flint 7H 7
Marsh Vw. CH5: Con Q 1J 23
Martin Cl. CH2: Mos 7J 17
Martin Rd. CH2: Mos 7J 17
Marton Rd. CH4: Brou 6G 35
Masefield Dr. CH1: Blac 2E 26
Masonic Pl. CH1: Ches 4D 44
Mason St. CH1: Ches 6J 27 (2B 44)
Matthew Cl. CH2: Ches 6B 28
Maude St. CH5: Con Q 1H 23
Maxwell Av. CH5: Man 5B 24
Maxwell Cl. CH7: Buck 4E 32
Maxwell Dr. CH7: Lees 5B 40
Maydor Av. CH4: Salt F 2C 36
Mayfield Av. CH7: Buck 5B 32
Mayfield M. CH7: Buck 4C 32
Mayfield Rd. CH1: Blac 3D 26
Maytree Av. CH3: Ches 6D 28
Meadow Av. CH7: Drury 3G 33
Meadowbank CH8: Holw 3D 4
Meadow-Bank Cl. CH6: Flint 2F 11
Meadow Cl. CH1: Moll 6F 17
Meadowcroft CH1: Saug 6B 16
CH4: High K 3E 42
Meadow Fld. Rd. CH4: Ches 4G 37
Meadow La. CH3: Hunt 7H 43
LL12: Burt 7H 43
Meadow Pl. CH7: Mold 5F 31
Meadow Ri. CH4: Penf 3J 41
Meadow Rd. CH4: Brou 5F 35
Meadows, The CH5: Shot 3K 23
CH6: Flint 1G 11
Meadowside CH5: Ewl 7J 23
CH7: Mold 3E 30
Meadowside M. CH1: Ches 4H 27
Meadows La. CH1: Saug 7A 16
CH4: Ches 2A 38 (7D 44)
Meadows Pl. CH4: Ches 1A 38
Meadowsway CH2: Upton 7K 17
Meadow Vw. CH5: Sea 2E 24
CH6: Bag 6H 33
Meadowview Ct. CH5: Dob 5K 33
Mechanics La. CH5: Pen 4C 24
Medlar Cl. CH4: Ches 4F 37
Megabowl
Chester 5F 27
Meg's La. CH7: Buck 6D 32
Melbourne Rd. CH1: Blac 4C 26
CH5: Shot 5C 32
Melbreck Av. CH5: Haw 7J 23
Melford Pl. CH5: Con Q 4F 23
Melin-y-Dre CH8: G'fld 2F 5
Melkridge Cl. CH2: Ches 5C 28
Melrose Av. CH3: Ches 6C 28
CH5: Shot 4K 23
Melverley Dr. CH1: Blac 4C 26
Melwood Cl. CH4: Penf 1J 41
Menhuin Ho. CH7: Ches 3K 27
Mercer Way CH4: Ches 3F 37
Mercia Dr. CH7: M Isa 4K 31
Mercia Sq. CH1: Ches 4C 44
Mercury Ct. CH1: Ches 6E 26
Merecroft CH3: Ches 7C 28
Merllyn Av. CH5: Con Q 1F 23
Merllyn Cl. CH6: Bag 4C 6
Merllyn La. CH6: Bag 4C 6
Merton Dr. CH4: Ches 5F 37
Mertyn Downing La. CH8: Whit 1A 4
Mertyn La. CH8: Carm 1B 4
Meynell Pl. CH1: Blac 3G 27
Micklegate CH2: Mick T 7G 19

MICKLE TRAFFORD 7G 19
Middlecroft CH3: Guil S 3G 29
Middle La. CH4: High K 5B 42
Middle Mill Rd. CH7: Nor 1C 20
Middle Row CH6: Bag 4C 6
    (off Foel Gron)
Midlothian Ho. CH1: Ches 3E 44
Milborne Cl. CH2: Upton 3A 28
Milford St. CH7: Mold 4F 31
Military Mus. 1J 37 (6B 44)
    (not continuous)
Millais Cl. CH5: Con Q 7E 12
Millbank Ct. CH3: Ches 6B 28
    (off Hoole La.)
Mill Cl. CH2: Upton 2K 27
Mill Clft. CH6: Flint 2J 11
Mill Cross CH3: Wav 4K 39
    (off Eggbridge La.)
Millers Cl. CH3: Wav 5J 39
Millfield La. CH3: Saig 7H 39
Millford St. CH7: Mold 4F 31
Mill La. CH7: Mold 3J 27
  CH5: Con Q 2J 23
  CH7: Buck 4D 32
Millstone Pk. CH4: Penf 2J 41
Mill St. CH4: Ches 1K 37 (7D 44)
Mill Vw. Rd. CH5: Shot 2J 23
Millway CH3: Wav 4K 39
Mill Wharf CH3: Wav 4K 39
Milton Rd. CH1: Blac 2F 27
Milton St. CH1: Ches 6K 27 (3D 44)
MILWR 7G 5
Milwr Rd. CH8: Pen H, Milwr 7G 5
Min Awel CH6: Flint 3H 11
Minerva Av. CH1: Ches 6E 26
Minerva Ct. CH1: Ches 6E 26
Minfordd Flds. CH7: G'nydd 7B 30
Moel Fammau Rd. CH7: New B 2J 31
Moel Ganol CH7: M Isa 4K 31
  CH7: Mold 5D 30
Moel Gron CH7: M Isa 4K 31
Moel Parc CH6: Flint 3H 11
Moel Vw. Dr. CH7: Nor H 4B 22
Moel Vw. Rd. CH7: Buck 6D 32
  CH7: M Isa 5A 32
Moelwyn Cl. CH7: Bryn B 3A 32
Mold Bus. Pk. CH7: Mold 7F 31
Mold Castle (ruins) 4E 30
MOLD COMMUNITY HOSPITAL 4E 30
Mold Ind. Est. CH7: Mold 7G 31
Mold Rd. CH4: Brou 6D 34
  CH5: Con Q 2F 23
  CH5: Ewl 7F 23
  CH5: Queen 3B 24
  CH7: Buck 5J 31
  CH7: M Isa 5J 31
  CH7: Nor 2B 22
  CH7: Pont 7G 41
  LL12: Cae 7G 41
Moldsdale Rd. CH7: Mold 5G 31
Mold Sports Cen. 6F 31
Mold Way CH5: Ewl 6G 23
MOLD (YR WYDDGRUG) 4F 31
MOLLINGTON 5F 17
Mollington Ct. CH1: Ches 6E 16
Monastery Rd. CH8: B'ford, Holy, Pant . .5A 4
Monet Cl. CH5: Con Q 7E 12
Montrose Ct. CH4: Ches 2F 37
Monza Cl. CH7: Buck 5B 32
  CH7: Nor H 4D 22
Moor Av. CH8: Holw 3C 4
Moor Cres. CH4: Low K 1H 43
MOOR CROFT 2J 31
Moor Cft. CH7: New B 2J 31
Moorcroft Av. CH3: Gt Bou 7D 28
Moorcroft Cl. CH3: Gt Bou 7D 28
Moorcroft Cres. CH3: Guil S 4E 28
Moorcroft M. CH4: Salt 3D 36
Moorefields CH7: Buck 5E 32
Moorfield Cl. CH5: Aston 5K 23
Moorfield Rd. CH5: Aston 6K 23
Moorfields CH8: Holw 3D 4
Moorhouse Cl. CH2: Ches 3K 27
Moorings, The CH3: Chris 2G 39
Moor La. CH3: Row 4J 39
  CH4: High K 4F 43
  CH4: Low K, High K 1G 43
  CH5: Haw 1C 34
  CH8: Holw 3C 4
Morgan Ol. OH1. Dlac 2F 27
Morley Av. CH5: Con Q 2G 23
Morley Cl. CH2: Mick T 7H 19
Mornington Cres. CH7: Drury 4G 33
Mortlake Cres. CH3: Ches 7C 28
Morton Rd. CH1: Blac 4E 26
Moses Ct. CH1: Ches 3E 44
Moss Bank CH1: Ches 4J 27
Moss Gro. CH4: Salt 3E 36
Mossley Ct. CH5: Haw 1A 34
MOSTON .6J 17
Moston Rd. CH2: Mos, Upton 6J 17

Mostyn Pl. CH1: Blac 2E 26
Mostyn Rd. CH8: G'fld 1G 5
Mostyn St. CH5: Shot 2K 23
Mount, The CH3: Ches 7B 28
  CH8: Milwr 7G 5
Mountain Vw. CH4: Salt 3E 36
Mountain Vw. Av. CH7: M Isa 4A 32
Mountain Vw. Cl. CH5: Con Q 4F 23
Mount Cl. CH7: M Isa 5K 31
Mountfield Rd. CH5: Aston 5K 23
Mount Pl. CH3: Ches 6B 28
MOUNT PLEASANT 2G 11
Mt. Pleasant CH4: Ches 2G 11
Mt. Pleasant Av. CH6: Flint 2G 11
Mt. Pleasant Rd. CH7: Drury 3F 33
Mt. Tabor Cl. CH4: Penym 7K 33
Mount Wlk. CH6: Flint 1G 11
    (off Duke St.)
Mountway CH3: Wav 5J 39
Muirfield Rd. CH7: Buck 4C 32
Muir Rd. CH1: Blac 5E 26
Mumforth Wlk. CH6: Flint 1G 11
    (off Duke St.)
Music Hall Pas. CH1: Ches 4C 44
Music Hall Pl. CH1: Ches 7K 27 (4C 44)
Muspratt Wlk. CH6: Flint 1G 11
    (off Sydney St.)
MWDWL-EITHIN 4A 4
MYNYDD .1J 31
MYNYDD ISA 4A 32
Myrica Gro. CH2: Ches 5D 28
Myrtle Av. CH4: High K 3E 42
Myrtle Gro. CH2: Ches 5D 28
Myrtle La. CH8: Holy 5G 5
Myrtle St. CH7: Buck 4B 32

N

NAID-Y-MARCH 5B 4
NANT, THE 5A 20
Nant Derw CH7: Mold 5D 30
Nant Eos CH8: Holw 3D 4
Nant Garmon CH7: Mold 5E 30
Nant Glyn CH7: Buck 6D 32
NANT MAWR 5C 32
Nant Mawr Ct. CH7: Buck 6C 32
    (off Farm Rd.)
  CH7: Buck 5C 32
    (Nant Mawr Cres.)
Nant Mawr Cres. CH7: Buck 5C 32
Nant Mawr Rd. CH7: Buck 5C 32
Nant Peris CH1: Blac 5D 26
Nant Rd. CH5: Con Q 7F 13
  CH8: Pen H 7A 6
Nant Vw. Ct. CH7: Buck 6C 32
Nant y Coed CH8: Holy 4G 5
Nant-y-Coed CH7: Mold 6E 30
Nant-y-Glyn CH6: Bag 3B 6
Naomi Cl. CH1: Blac 3D 26
Napier Rd. CH7: Mos 7J 17
Narrow La. CH8: B'ford 6C 4
Nefyn Cl. CH5: Con Q 1E 22
Neighbourhood Cen.
  CH5: Con Q 1E 22
Nelson St. CH1: Ches 6A 28 (2E 44)
  CH5: Shot 2K 23
Nercwys Rd. CH7: Mold, Nerc 7G 31
Neston Dr. CH2: Ches 3K 27
Neston Vw. CH6: Bag 4C 6
Neville Dr. CH3: Ches 7D 28
Neville Rd. CH3: Ches 7D 28
Nevin Cl. CH1: Blac 5D 26
NEW BRIGHTON (PENTRE CYTHRAUL) . .2J 31
New Brighton Rd. CH6: Bag 4K 5
  CH7: New B, S'ton 7H 21
Newbury Rd. CH4: Ches 3F 37
Newby Wlk. CH5: Con Q 7E 12
New Crane Bank CH1: Ches 7H 27
New Crane St. CH1: Ches 6H 27 (4A 44)
Newcroft CH1: Saug 5B 16
Newgate Row CH1: Ches 7K 27 (4C 44)
Newgate St. CH1: Ches 7K 27 (5C 44)
Newgate Wlk. CH1: Ches 7K 27 (5C 44)
Newhall Ct. CH2: Upton 2A 28
Newhall La. CH2: Upton 2A 28
Newhall Rd. CH2: Upton 2A 28
New Pk. Rd. CH5: Aston 4J 23
New Rd. CH5: Dob 5K 33
  CH5: Ewl 1E 1
New Roskell Sq. CH6: Flint 7H 7
Newry Ct. CH2: Ches 4K 27
Newry Pk. CH2: Ches 4K 27
Newry Pk. E. CH2: Ches 4K 27
New Shop Pde. CH8: G'fld 1G 5
    (off Greenfield Rd.)
New St. CH5: Con Q 1H 23
  CH7: Mold 5F 31
Newtech Sq. CH5: Dee I 5D 14
Newthorn Pl. CH7: Buck 5D 32
NEWTON .3B 28

Newton Cl. CH7: Nor H 4B 22
Newton Dr. CH7: Drury 4H 33
Newton Hall Cl. CH2: Ches 3B 28
Newton Hall Dr. CH2: Ches 3B 28
Newton Hollows CH2: Ches 4B 28
Newton Ho. CH2: Ches 3B 28
Newton La. CH2: Ches 3A 28
Newton Pk. Vw. CH2: Ches 4K 27
Newtown Cl. CH1: Ches 6K 27 (2D 44)
New Union St. CH5: Con Q 7F 13
Nicholas Ct. CH1: Ches 7J 27 (5A 44)
Nicholas St. CH1: Ches 7J 27 (5B 44)
Nicholas St. M. CH1: Ches 7J 27 (5A 44)
Nickolson Cl. CH2: Mick T 7H 19
Nield Ct. CH2: Upton 1K 27
Nook, The CH2: Ches 4A 28
  CH3: Guil S 4E 28
  CH4: Salt 3E 36
  CH5: Man 6B 24
Norfolk Rd. CH2: Ches 4B 28
Norley Dr. CH3: Ches 7E 28
Normanby Dr. CH5: Con Q 2F 23
Normandy Rd. CH2: Mos 6J 17
Norman St. CH5: Shot 4K 23
Norman Way CH1: Blac 3E 26
Norris Rd. CH1: Blac 3E 26
Northern Pathway CH4: Ches 1A 38 (7E 44)
Northgate Arena Leisure Cen. 5K 27 (2C 44)
Northgate Av. CH2: Ches 5K 27 (1C 44)
Northgate Row CH1: Ches 4B 44
Northgate St. CH1: Ches 6J 27 (3B 44)
North Gro. CH5: Sea 2E 24
Northop Cl. CH5: Con Q 2F 23
Northop Country Pk. Golf Course 4J 21
NORTHOP HALL 4B 22
NORTHOP (LLAN-EURGAIN) 3G 11
Northop Rd. CH6: Flint, Flint M 5F 11
  CH7: Nor 5F 11
North Rd. CH5: Dee I 5G 13
  CH8: Holy 5E 4
North St. CH3: Ches 7C 28
  CH4: Salt F 2B 36
  CH5: Sand 5E 24
  CH5: Shot 3K 23
Northway CH4: Ches 2G 37
Norton Av. CH4: Salt 3D 36
Norton Rd. CH3: Ches 6E 28
Norwood Dr. CH4: Ches 3H 37
Nuns Rd. CH1: Ches 7J 27 (5A 44)
Nurseries, The CH6: Flint 2F 11

O

Oak Bank La. CH2: Hoole V 1E 28
Oak Cl. CH5: Con Q 7F 13
Oakdale Cl. CH4: Brou 6F 35
Oak Dr. CH4: High K 3E 42
  CH7: Buck 2D 32
  CH7: Lees 5B 40
OAKENHOLT 3A 12
Oakenholt La. CH6: Oak 5A 12
  CH7: Nor 5A 12
Oakfield Av. CH2: Upton 7A 18
Oakfield Dr. CH2: Upton 7A 18
Oakfield Rd. CH1: Blac 4C 26
  CH5: Haw 7J 23
  CH7: Buck 5E 32
Oak Gro. CH6: Flint 5D 6
Oak Ho. CH2: Ches 3J 27
Oaklands CH3: Guil S 3G 29
Oak La. CH7: Hoole V 2E 28
Oaklea Av. CH2: Ches 4B 28
Oakley Rd. CH5: Man 6C 24
Oakmere Dr. CH3: Gt Bou 1D 38
Oak Pk. CH7: Lees 5B 40
Oak Rd. CH4: Ches 3F 37
Oaks, The CH5: Haw 6F 35
Oaks Dr. CH2: Upton 1K 27
Oaktree Bus. Pk. CH7: Mold 7H 31
Oak Tree Cl. CH5: Shot 4J 23
  CH7: Buck 4E 32
Oaktree Ct. CH2: Ches 5C 28
Oakwood Cl. CH7: Mold 3E 30
Oakwood Vs. CH5: Con Q 2G 23
Ochr y Waen CH7: Buck 3C 32
Odeon Cinema
  Foregate St. 4D 44
  Hunter St. 6J 27 (3B 44)
Old Aston Hill CH51 Ewl 5J 23
    (Fern Gro.)
  CH5: Ewl 6H 23
    (Liverpool Rd.)
Old Bagillt Rd. CH6: Bag 5G 5
  CH8: Holy 5G 5
Old Bank La. CH7: Buck 6D 32
Old Chester Rd. CH5: Ewl 6H 23
  CH8: Holy 6F 5
Oldfield Cres. CH4: Ches 4F 37
Oldfield Dr. CH3: Ches 6E 28
Oldfield M. CH3: Ches 6E 28

Old Hall Gdns. CH2: Ches 5A 28
Old Hall Pk. CH3: Guil S 3H 29
Old Hall Pl. CH1: Ches 7J 27 (5B 44)
Old Hall Rd. CH5: Haw 7J 23
Old Hope Rd. CH4: Penym 7A 34
    CH5: Dob 5K 33
Old Liverpool Rd. CH5: Ewl 7G 23
Old London Rd. CH6: Bag 4B 6
    (Bron-y-Wern)
    CH6: Bag 5D 6
    (Tyddyn Messham)
    CH6: Flint 7E 6
Old Mill Ct. CH2: Upton 2K 27
Old Orchard, The CH5: Haw 1B 34
Old Paper Mill La. CH6: Oak 4A 12
Old Pearl La. CH3: Ches 7D 28
Old Port Sq. CH1: Ches 6H 27
Old Post Office Yd. CH1: Ches 4C 44
Old Sealand Rd. CH1: Sea 2J 25
Old Seals Way CH1: Ches 5G 27
OLD WARREN 5C 34
Old Woman's La. CH3: Chris 2F 39
Old Wrexham Rd. CH4: Ches 2J 37
Onnen CH6: Flint 3H 11
Onslow Rd. CH1: Blac 4D 26
On The Air Broadcasting Mus. 5C 44
Orchard, The CH3: Gt Bou 1C 38
    CH7: Lees 6C 40
Orchard Cl. CH2: Ches 3K 27
    CH5: Man 5B 24
    CH7: Buck 5D 32
Orchard Ct. CH3: Ches 7C 28
Orchard Cft. CH3: Guil S 3G 29
Orchard Lea CH5: Ewl 7E 22
Orchards, The CH4: Salt 3D 36
    CH5: Con Q 4E 22
Orchard St. CH1: Ches 6H 27 (2A 44)
Orchard Way CH5: Gard C 1D 24
    CH7: Mold 3E 30
Orchid Cl. CH3: Hunt 3D 38
Ormonde Rd. CH2: Ches 4J 27
Ormonde St. CH1: Ches 6A 28 (2E 44)
Osborne Ct. CH5: Con Q 7G 13
Oulton Av. CH2: Upton 1A 28
Oulton Pl. CH1: Ches 6K 27 (2C 44)
Overdale Av. CH7: M Isa 5J 31
Overlea Cres. CH5: Haw 6A 24
Overlea Dr. CH5: Haw 6A 24
Overleigh Ct. CH4: Ches 2K 37
    CH7: Buck 4B 32
Overleigh Rd. CH4: Ches 2J 37 (7C 44)
Overleigh Ter. CH4: Ches 2J 37 (7B 44)
Overton Cl. CH7: Buck 5E 32
Overwood Av. CH1: Moll 6E 16
Overwood La. CH1: Blac 4C 26
    CH1: Moll 6D 16
Owen Cl. CH1: Blac 2E 26
Oxford Rd. CH4: Ches 3F 37

P

Padarn Cl. CH4: Salt 4D 36
Paddock, The CH4: Ches 2H 37
    CH5: Man 6B 24
Paddock Rd. CH4: Ecc 7A 38
Paddock Row CH1: Ches 7K 27 (5C 44)
Paddock Way CH4: High K 3E 42
    CH7: G'nydd 7B 30
PADESWOOD 2D 40
Padeswood Dr. CH7: Pade 7G 33
Padeswood Lake Rd. CH7: Pade 2D 40
Padeswood Rd. CH7: Buck 5D 32
Padeswood Rd. Sth.
    CH7: Buck, Pade 1C 40
Palace Cl. CH6: Flint 1E 10
Palatine Cl. CH1: Blac 2D 26
Palgrave Cl. CH1: Blac 3G 27
Palmerston Cl. CH1: Ches 4H 27
Palmerston Cres. CH5: Haw 1H 33
PANTASAPH 5A 4
PANT-GLAS 4A 30
Pant Glas CH7: S'ton 7G 21
Pant Isa CH7: S'ton 7G 21
Panton Pl. CH2: Ches 5B 28
    CH8: Holy 5F 5
Panton Rd. CH2: Ches 5B 28
Pant Ucha CH7: S'ton 7G 21
Pant y Fownog Dr. CH7: Buck 5B 32
PANT Y GOF 6A 10
Paper Mill La. CH6: Oak 3A 12
Parade, The CH1: Blac 3E 26
Paradise CH4: Ches 1K 37 (7D 44)
Paradise La. CH5: Ewl 1H 33
Parc Alum CH7: Mold 4G 31
Parc Bryn Castell CH5: Con Q 4E 22
Parc Capel CH8: Lixm 7B 8
Parc Hendy CH7: Mold 5D 30
Parc Issa CH7: Bryn B 3A 32
Parc Plas Aney CH7: Mold 5D 30

Park, The CH3: Chris 1G 39
    CH7: Mold 5E 30
Park and Ride
    Boughton Heath 1E 38
    Sealand Road 6D 26
    Upton (Zoo, The) 6K 17
    Wrexham Road 6G 37
Park Av. CH1: Saug 5A 16
    CH4: High K 3D 42
    CH4: Salt 3E 36
    CH5: Haw 2A 24
    CH5: Shot 2A 24
    CH6: Flint 1H 11
    CH7: Bryn B 4K 31
    CH7: Mold 4E 30
    CH8: Carm 3C 4
Park Ct. CH1: Ches 4E 44
Park Cres. CH4: Penf 3J 41
    CH8: Carm 3B 4
Park Dr. CH2: Ches 4C 28
    CH8: Carm 3B 4
Park Dr. Sth. CH2: Ches 4C 28
Parkers Bldgs. CH1: Ches 7A 28 (3E 44)
Parker's Yd. CH1: Ches 6C 44
Parkfield Rd. CH4: Brou 6G 35
Parkgate Ct. CH1: Ches 4H 27
Parkgate Rd. CH1: Moll, Ches 7E 16 (1A 44)
    CH1: Saug 3B 16
    CH1: Wood 1J 15
Park Gro. CH5: Con Q 2H 23
Park Hall Rd. CH8: G'fld 2G 5
Parkhill Rd. CH5: Con Q 1J 23
Park Ho. M. CH7: Mold 5F 31
Park La. CH1: L'ton 5H 29
    CH4: Penf 3J 41
    CH8: Holy 5F 5
Park Rd. CH6: Bag 5C 6
    CH7: Buck 4E 32
    CH8: Carm 3B 4
Park Rd. W. CH4: Ches 2G 37
Parkside CH7: Buck 4D 32
Parkside Av. CH5: Con Q 2E 22
Park St. CH1: Ches 7K 27 (5D 44)
Park Vw. CH7: Drury 4H 33
    CH7: Nor 3J 21
Park Wlk. CH2: Ches 4K 27
    CH7: Buck 4E 32
    CH8: Holy 4G 5
Park Way CH1: Saug 6A 16
Parkway CH5: Dee I 5B 14
    CH7: Mold 5F 31
Parkway Bus. Cen.
    CH5: Dee I 5C 14
Park W. CH1: Ches 6E 26
Parsons La. CH2: Ches 1H 27
Pastures, The CH4: Penf 3J 41
Pathway, The CH4: Brou 5F 35
Patten Cl. CH5: Ewl 1G 33
Pavilion Leisure Cen., The 7G 7
Pavilions, The CH4: Ches 6H 37
Peach Fld. CH3: Gt Bou 2D 38
Pearl La. CH3: Ches 6D 28
    CH3: L'ton 7E 28
Pear Tree Cl. CH5: Shot 4J 23
Pear Tree Way CH2: Ches 3B 28
Peckforton Way CH2: Upton 2A 28
Peel Ter. CH1: Ches 6A 28 (2E 44)
Pemba Dr. CH7: Buck 4E 32
Pemberton Rd. CH1: Ches 6J 27 (3B 44)
Pembroke Cl. CH4: Ches 3A 38
    CH5: Queen 4B 24
Pembry Ri. CH5: Con Q 7E 12
Penfold Hey CH2: Upton 1K 27
Penfold Way CH4: D'ton 6J 43
Pengwladys Av. CH5: Con Q 3F 23
Penlan Dr. CH5: Haw 6A 24
Pen Lan La. CH8: Halk 3A 10
Penley Rd. CH7: Buck 5E 32
Pen Lon CH6: Bag 3K 5
Penmon Cl. CH1: Blac 5D 26
Pennant St. CH1: Ches 1H 23
Penny Bank Cl. CH4: Brou 6E 34
Penrhos Ct. CH5: Con Q 4E 22
Penrhyn CH8: Holy 4H 5
Pensby Av. CH2: Ches 3K 27
Pentland Cl. CH3: Ches 6C 28
PENTRE 5H 31
Pentre, The CH6: Bag 3B 6
    (off Gadlys La.)
PENTRE CYTHRAUL 2J 31
PENTRE FFWRNDAN 2J 11
PENTRE HALKYN 5J 9
Pentre Hill CH6: Flint M 6F 11
Pentre Ind. Est. CH5: Pen 4D 24
Pentre La. CH7: Buck 2C 32
Pentre Rd. CH8: Pen H, Halk 5J 9
Pentre Ter. CH6: Flint M 6G 11
PENTROBIN 4K 33
PEN-UCHA'R PLWYF 5D 8
Pen-y-Ball Hill CH8: Holy 6D 4

Pen-y-Ball St. CH8: Holy 5E 4
PEN-Y-BALL TOP 5D 4
Pen-y-Bryn CH6: Flint 3H 11
    CH7: Mold 5E 30
    CH7: S'ton 7G 21
Pen y Coed Rd. CH7: Drury 3G 33
PENYFFORD 2J 41
Penyffordd Station (Rail) 3H 41
Pen-y-Garreg Cl. CH7: Bryn B 4A 32
Pen-y-Glyn CH6: Bag 3B 6
    CH6: Flint M 6F 11
Pen-y-Llan St. CH5: Con Q 7F 13
Pen-y-Lon CH7: M Isa 5J 31
PEN-Y-MAES 4G 5
Pen y Maes CH7: Buck 5C 32
Penymaes CH7: M Isa 4K 31
Pen-y-Maes Gdns. CH8: Holy 5G 5
Pen-y-Maes Rd. CH8: G'fld, Holy 5F 5
PENYMYNYDD 1K 41
Penymynydd Rd. CH4: Penf, Penym 2J 41
Pen-y-Nant CH6: Bag 3B 6
    (off Nant-y-Glyn)
PEN Y PARC 7A 10
Pen y Parc Bungs. CH7: Rhos 7A 10
Pen-y-Pentre CH7: S'ton 7H 21
Pen-y-Pylle CH8: B'ford 1G 9
PEN-YR-ALLT 2E 40
Pepper Row CH1: Ches 5C 44
Pepper St. CH1: Ches 7K 27 (5C 44)
    CH3: Chris 1F 39
Percival Cl. CH2: Mos 7J 17
Percival Rd. CH2: Mos 6J 17
Percy Rd. CH4: Ches 2K 37 (7D 44)
Perrins Wlk. CH6: Flint 1G 11
    (off Sydney St.)
Philip St. CH5: Sand 6E 24
Phillips Rd. CH1: Blac 5D 26
Phillip St. CH2: Ches 5A 28
Phoenix St. CH5: Sand 5E 24
Pickering St. CH2: Ches 5A 28
Pickmere Dr. CH3: Gt Bou 1D 38
PICTON 4F 19
Picton Gorse La. CH2: Hoole V, Pic 1D 38
Picton La. CH2: Pic, Mick T 2E 18
    CH2: Stoak, Wer 1C 18
Picton Valley CH2: Pic 4E 18
Pierce St. CH5: Queen 3B 24
Pierpoint La. CH1: Ches 7J 27 (5C 44)
Pigeon Ho. La. LL12: Hope 7J 41
Pilgrims Cl. CH7: Nor 3G 21
Pine Crest CH6: Flint 2E 10
Pine Gdns. CH2: Upton 2J 27
Pine Gro. CH2: Ches 4D 28
    CH7: M Isa 5A 32
Pine Ho. CH2: Ches 3H 27
Pines, The CH5: Haw 2H 33
Pinetree Cl. CH4: Brou 6F 35
Pinewood Av. CH5: Con Q 1G 23
Pinewood Rd. CH7: Drury 4H 33
Pinfold Cl. CH4: Ches 3A 38
Pinfold Ind. Est. CH7: Buck 2D 32
Pinfold La. CH4: Ches 3K 37
    CH7: Buck, Nor H 5B 22
    (not continuous)
Pinfold Workshops CH7: Buck 2D 32
Pingot Cft. CH3: Gt Bou 2D 38
PIPER'S ASH 4D 28
Pipers Cl. CH4: Ches 4D 28
Pipers La. CH2: Ches 4D 28
Pippins Cl. CH5: Shot 3J 23
Pistyll CH8: Milwr 7G 5
Pitmans La. CH5: Haw 7A 24
Plas Dewi CH8: Holy 4F 5
    (off Well St.)
Plas Dinas CH1: Blac 5D 26
Plas Gwenfrewi CH8: Holy 4E 4
    (off New Rd.)
Plas Newton La. CH2: Ches 3A 28
Plas-yn-Rhos CH4: Penf 3H 41
Platt La. CH4: Penf 5J 41
Pleasant Vw. CH4: Penym 1K 41
Plemstall Cl. CH2: Mick T 7H 19
Plemstall La. CH2: Mick T 6H 19
Plemstall Way CH2: Mick T 6H 19
Plough La. CH3: Chris 2G 39
    CH5: Aston 4K 23
Plumley Cl. CH3: Ches 7E 28
Plum Ter. CH1: Ches 6J 27 (2A 44)
Plymouth St. CH5: Shot 2J 23
PONTBLYDDYN 5D 40
PONTERWYL 5G 31
PONTYBODKIN 7C 40
Pontybodkin Hill CH7: Lees, Ponty 7C 40
Poplar Av. CH5: Shot 4K 23
Poplar Cl. CH5: Con Q 2G 23
Poplar Gro. CH5: Ewl 6G 23
Poplar Ho. CH1: Ches 6F 27
Poplar Rd. CH4: Ches 4F 37
Poplars, The CH5: Haw 2H 33
Poplars Est. CH8: Pen H 4H 9
Poppyfield Dr. CH4: Penf 2J 41

Porters Cft. CH3: Guil S 3H 29
Post Office La. CH8: Pant 5A 4
Potters Way CH7: Buck 4C 32
Powell Rd. CH7: Buck 6C 32
Powell's Orchard CH4: Ches 2J 37
Powey La. CH1: Moll 3B 16
Powys Cl. CH5: Queen 4B 24
   CH7: Buck 3E 32
Powys Ct. CH1: Ches 6J 27 (3A 44)
Precinct, The CH7: Buck 5D 32
Precinct Way CH7: Buck 6D 32
Pren Av. CH7: M Isa 5A 32
PRENBRIGOG 5B 32
Pren Hill CH7: Buck .5B 32
Prenton Pl. CH4: Ches 2A 38 (7E 44)
Prescot St. CH2: Ches 5B 28
Pretoria St. CH1: Ches 2K 37 (7D 44)
Primrose Cl. CH3: Hunt 3C 38
   CH7: Nor H 4D 22
Primrose Hill CH5: Con Q 7H 13
Primrose St. CH1: Ches 7G 13
Prince of Wales Av. CH6: Flint 1G 11
   CH8: Holy 4G 5
Prince of Wales Ct. CH7: Buck 5F 33
                               (off Brook St.)
Prince's Av. CH1: Ches 6A 28
Princes Dr. CH6: Flint 3H 11
Princess Av. CH7: Buck 3E 32
Princess St. CH1: Ches 7J 27 (4B 44)
Princes St. CH5: Con Q 1G 23
   CH6: Flint 1H 11
Prince William Av. CH5: Sand 5F 25
Prince William Ct. CH5: Ewl 7J 23
Prince William Gdns. CH5: Man 6C 24
Priors Cl. CH5: Aston 4J 23
Priory Cl. CH1: Ches 4J 27
   CH4: Penf 3H 41
Priory Pl. CH1: Ches 7K 27 (4D 44)
Private Wlk. CH3: Ches 1C 38
Promised Land La. CH3: Row 4G 39
Prospect Cl. CH5: Ewl 6J 23
Prosser Rd. CH2: Mos 6H 17
Provan Way CH1: Blac 3D 26
Providence Ct. CH8: G'fld 2H 5
Pulford La. CH4: D'ton 6J 43
Pulford Rd. CH1: Blac 3E 26
PWLL-CLAI 2F 9
PWLL GLAS 5E 30
Pwll Glas CH7: Mold 4E 30
PWLL-MELYN 7E 8
Pwll y Hwyaden CH6: Flint 4H 11
Pyecroft St. CH4: Ches 2K 37

Q

Quadrant, The CH1: Ches 6D 26
Quaker Meeting Ho. CH1: Ches 4D 44
Quarry Cl. CH4: Ches 2J 37
   CH7: Nor H 4B 22
Quarry La. CH3: Chris 2F 39
   CH3: Wav 6J 39
   CH5: Con Q 2G 23
   CH7: S'ton 7G 21
Quay Bus. Pk. CH5: Con Q 6G 13
Quay La. CH5: Con Q 7G 13
Queens Av. CH1: Ches 6A 28
   CH5: Con Q 7F 13
   CH5: Sand 5E 24
   CH6: Flint 2H 11
Queensbury Dr. CH6: Flint 1E 10
Queenscourt CH4: Ches 1A 38
Queens Cres. CH2: Upton 1A 28
Queens Dr. CH4: Ches 1A 38 (6E 44)
   CH7: Buck 5D 32
QUEENSFERRY 3B 24
Queensferry Ind. Est. CH5: Pen 4D 24
QUEEN'S PARK 1K 37 (7D 44)
Queen's Pk. Ho. CH8: Ches 7D 44
Queen's Pk. Rd. CH4: Ches 4D 30
Queen's Pk. Vw. CH4: Ches 1K 37 (7D 44)
Queens Pl. CH1: Ches 6K 27 (3D 44)
Queens Rd. CH1: Ches 6A 28
   CH5: Gard C 1D 24
   CH8: G'fld 1F 5
   CH3: Ches 6D 28
Queens St. CH6: Flint 1H 11
Queen St. CH1: Ches 6K 27 (3D 44)
   CH5: Queen 5D 24
   CH7: Lees 6C 40
Queen's Way CH4: Brou 5F 35
Queensway CH2: Ches 3B 28
   CH5: Shot 2J 23

R

Radford Cl. CH5: Con Q 1J 23
Radnor Cl. CH5: Queen 4B 24

Rodnor Dr. CH4: Cheo 1C 37
Raewood Av. CH5: Haw 1H 33
Raikes La. CH7: Mold, S'ton 7F 21
Railway Ter. CH5: Con Q 7G 13
                           (off Church Hill)
   CH5: Sand 5F 25
Rake La. CH2: Chor B, Lit S 3K 17
   CH3: Chris 1J 39
   CH4: Ecc 7J 37
   CH5: Haw 2D 34
   WA6: Dun H 1K 19
Rake Way CH1: Saug 7A 16
Ramsden Ct. CH4: Ches 5F 37
Ranwonath Ct. CH2: Ches 5K 27 (1C 44)
Raven Sq. CH6: Flint 7G 7
Rawson Rd. CH1: Blac 5E 26
Raymond St. CH1: Ches 6J 27 (3A 44)
Rayon Rd. CH8: G'fld 3H 5
Recorder's Steps CH1: Ches 6C 44
Rectors La. CH3: Pen 5D 24
Rectory Cl. CH6: Flint 2G 11
Rectory Dr. CH5: Haw 1B 34
Red Hall Av. CH5: Con Q 1H 23
Red Hall Pct. CH5: Con Q 1G 23
Redhill Rd. CH4: Ches 3F 37
Redland Cl. CH4: Ches 2G 37
Red Rd. CH7: Buck 3D 32
Redwood Cl. CH4: Salt 3E 36
Reece Cl. CH2: Mick T 7G 19
Reeces Ter. CH6: Bag 3C 6
Reeves Rd. CH3: Gt Bou 1D 38
Regency Ct. CH2: Mick T 7G 19
Regents Cl. CH3: Ches 6D 28
Reservoir Ter. CH3: Ches 6B 28
                       (off Richmond Ct.)
Reynolds Rd. CH6: Flint 5E 6
RHES-Y-CAE 7F 9
Rhodfa Cilcain CH7: Mold 6E 30
Rhodfa Mynydd CH7: Mold 6E 30
Rhodfa Wenlo CH8: G'fld 2F 5
Rhone Ct. CH3: Gt Bou 2C 38
Rhos Av. CH4: Penf .3H 41
RHOSESMOR 2A 20
Rhosesmor Ind. Est. CH7: Rhos 3A 20
Rhosesmor Rd. CH7: Nor 1C 20
   CH8: Halk 5A 10
Rhos Estyn LL12: Hope 7K 41
Rhoslan CH8: Holy 4G 5
Rhos Rd. CH4: Penf .3H 41
Rhoswen CH6: Flint .3H 11
Rhuddlan Cl. CH4: Salt 3E 36
Rhuddlan Rd. CH1: Blac 4D 26
   CH7: Buck 2E 32
Rhyd Osber CH7: Coed 7B 40
Rhydmwyn Rd. CH7: G'field 2A 30
Rhydymynydd CH8: B'ford 1D 8
Richard Hgts. CH6: Flint 7G 7
                       (off Feathers St.)
Richards Cft. CH3: Gt Bou 2C 38
Richmond Cl. CH3: Ches 6B 28
Richmond Cres. CH3: Ches 7E 28
Richmond M. CH2: Ches 6B 28
Richmond Rd. CH5: Con Q 2H 23
Ridgehill Dr. CH6: Bag 3B 6
Ridges La. CH3: Saig, Row, Wav 5E 38
Ridgeway, The CH5: Haw 6K 23
   CH7: Nor H 4B 22
   CH8: Milwr 7G 5
Ridgeway Cl. CH5: Con Q 2F 23
Ridings, The CH1: Saug 6A 16
Ring Rd. CH3: Gt Bou, Ches 4D 28
   CH5: Dee I 5G 13
Ringway CH3: Wav 4K 39
Riverbank CH6: Bag .4J 5
River La. CH4: Ches 2J 37 (7B 44)
   CH4: Salt 2D 36
River Rd. CH5: Dee I .6G 13
Riverside CH4: Salt 2C 36
Riverside Ct. CH3: Gt Bou 2B 38
   CH7: Pont 4D 40
Riverside Ind. Est. CH4: Salt 2E 36
Riverside Pk. CH5: Gard C 2D 24
Riversmead CH3: Hunt 4C 38
River Vw. CH5: Con Q 7F 13
   CH7: Mold 4G 31
Roadside CH3: Chris .1F 39
Robert's Ter. CH1: Ches 7H 27
Robinsons Cft. CH3: Gt Bou 2D 38
Rockcliffe CH7: Bryn B 3K 31
Rockcliff La. CH6: Kel 4C 12
Rock La. CH1: Ches 5J 27 (1D 44)
Rock Rd. CH5: Con Q 6G 13
Roebourne Ri. CH1: Blac 4D 26
Roman Amphitheatre 7K 27 (5D 44)
Roman Dr. CH1: Blac 2D 26
Romans Way CH6: Bag 5D 6
Roman Way CH7: Buck 5D 32
Roodee, The 1H 37 (6A 44)
Rookery, The CH4: Brou 6F 35
Ropewalks, The CH1: Ches 6H 27
                    (off Whipcord La.)

Rooodono Cl. CH2: Upton 7A 18
Rosehill CH8: Holy 5F 5
Rose La. CH7: Llong, M Isa 5K 31
Rosemary Cl. CH4: Brou 6G 35
Rosemary Wlk. CH6: Flint 1G 11
                          (off Sydney St.)
Rosewood Av. CH2: Ches 3K 27
Rosewood Gro. CH1: Saug 6B 16
   CH7: Drury 4H 33
Rosslyn Cl. CH5: Haw 6E 24
Rosslyn Rd. CH3: Ches 5D 28
Rothesay Rd. CH4: Ches 2G 37
ROUGHHILL 7E 36
Roughlyn Cres. CH4: Marl L 7E 36
Round Hill Mdw. CH3: Gt Bou 2D 38
Rowan Cl. CH7: Buck 5F 33
Rowan Gro. CH5: Con Q 6E 12
Rowan Pk. CH3: Chris 2G 39
Rowan Pl. CH2: Ches 4D 28
Rowan Rd. CH5: Aston 5J 23
Rowans, The CH4: Brou 6F 35
Rowcliffe Av. CH4: Ches 5G 37
Rowden Cres. CH5: Shot 2J 23
Rowden St. CH5: Shot 2J 23
Rowena Ct. CH2: Ches 5B 28
Rowlands Hgts. CH1: Ches 2E 44
Rowley's Dr. CH5: Shot 2K 23
Rowleys Pk. CH5: Shot 2A 24
ROWTON 4H 39
Rowton Bri. Rd. CH3: Chris 2G 39
Rowton La. CH3: Row 3G 39
Royal Ct. CH5: Con Q 7G 13
                         (off Tuscan Way)
Royal Dr. CH6: Flint .1E 10
Rufus Ct. CH1: Ches 6J 27 (3B 44)
Rufus Ct. Row CH1: Ches 3B 44
Rumney Cl. CH5: Con Q 4E 22
Rushfield Rd. CH4: Ches 4H 37
Rushton Dr. CH2: Upton 1A 28
Russell St. CH3: Ches 6A 28 (3E 44)
Ruthin Cl. CH7: Buck 3E 32
Ruthin Rd. CH7: Mold, G'nydd 7A 30
Rutland Cl. CH3: Ches 2F 23
Rutland Pl. CH2: Ches 3C 28
Rydal Dr. CH7: Buck .3E 32
Rydal Gro. CH4: Ches 3G 37
Ryeland Cl. CH5: Shot 1K 23

S

SAIGHTON 7H 39
Saighton La. CH3: Wav, Saig 7H 39
St Andrews Cl. CH5: Haw 1A 34
                          (off Friars Ct.)
St Andrews Dr. CH7: Buck 4C 32
St Andrews Wlk. CH2: Mick T 6H 19
St Annes CH1: Ches 6K 27 (2C 44)
St Annes Pl. CH1: Ches 2B 44
St Anne St. CH1: Ches 6K 27 (2C 44)
                      (not continuous)
St Bartholomews Ct. CH5: Sea 2J 25
St Bridgets Ct. CH4: Ches 3H 37
St Catherines Cl. CH6: Flint 1G 11
St Chads Hamlet CH1: Blac 4F 27
St Chad's Rd. CH1: Blac 4F 27
St Christophers Cl. CH2: Upton 7K 17
St Davids Cl. CH5: Ewl 6H 23
   CH7: Buck 3C 32
   CH6: Flint 3H 11
St David's Dr. CH5: Con Q 1F 23
   CH5: Shot 2K 23
St David's La. CH7: Mold 4G 31
ST DAVIDS PARK 1G 33
St Davids Pk. CH5: Ewl 1G 33
St David's Retail Pk. CH5: Con Q 2D 36
St David's Ter. CH4: Salt F 2C 36
St Deiniols Library & Gladstone Mus. 1A 34
St Edmunds Ter. CH8: G'fld 3F 5
                      (off Greenfield Rd.)
St Ethelwolds St. CH5: Shot 4K 23
St George's CH1: Ches 6K 27 (2D 44)
St George's Cres. CH3: Wav 4J 39
   CH4: Ches 1A 38 (7E 44)
St Giles CH3: Ches 7B 28
                      (off Sandy La.)
St Ives Pk. CH5: Sand 5E 24
St Ives Way CH5: Sand 5E 24
St James Av. CH2: Upton 1B 28
St James Cl. CH5: Haw 1A 34
St James Ct. CH5: Haw . . . . .off 10
St James Pl. CH8: Holw 4D 4
St James St. CH1: Ches 6K 27 (2D 44)
St Johns Cl. CH4: Penym 1K 41
   CH5: Haw 1K 33
   CH7: Buck 4D 32
St Johns Ct. CH1: Ches 4D 44
St John's Rear Rd. CH4: Ches 1A 38 (6E 44)
St John's Rd. CH4: Ches 1A 38 (6E 44)
St John St. CH1: Ches 7K 27 (4D 44)
St Mark's Av. CH5: Con Q 1F 23

St Mark's Rd. CH4: Ches 3F 37
St Martin's Way CH1: Ches 6J 27 (3A 44)
St Mary's Cl. CH7: Nor H 4B 22
St Mary's Dr. CH7: Nor H 4B 22
St Mary's Hill CH1: Ches 1K 37 (6C 44)
St Mary's M. CH7: Mold 4F 31
St Mary's Rd. CH4: D'ton 6J 43
St Mary's Way CH4: Brou 4G 35
St Mellor's Rd. CH7: Buck 4C 32
St Michael's Row CH1: Ches 7K 27 (5C 44)
St Michael's Sq. CH1: Ches 1G 33
St Olave St. CH1: Ches 1K 37 (6C 44)
St Oswald's Cl. CH1: Ches 6K 27 (2C 44)
St Oswald's Way CH1: Ches 6J 27 (2B 44)
St Pauls Cl. CH5: Haw 1A 34
                                            (off Friars Ct.)
St Peters Est. CH8: Holy 5G 5
St Peter's Pk. CH7: Nor 2G 21
St Peters Way CH2: Mick T 7H 19
St Thomas Ct. CH6: Flint M 6G 11
St Thomas Pathway
         CH1: Ches 7K 27 (4D 44)
St Werburgh Mt. CH1: Ches 4C 44
St Werburgh Row CH1: Ches 4C 44
St Werburgh St. CH1: Ches 7K 27 (4C 44)
Saith-Aelwyd Pk. CH8: Carm 3B 4
Salerno Rd. CH2: Mos 7H 17
Salisbury Av. CH4: Salt 3D 36
Salisbury St. CH1: Ches 5H 27
         CH5: Shot 2K 23
Salmon Leap CH4: Ches 1K 37 (6D 44)
Salter's La. CH2: Pic 7E 18
SALTNEY 3E 36
Saltney Bus. Cen. CH4: Salt 2F 37
Saltney Ferry Rd. CH4: Salt F 2B 36
Saltney Ter. CH4: Salt F 2B 36
Salusbury St. CH6: Flint 7H 7
Samuel St. CH1: Ches 6A 28 (3E 44)
Sandileigh CH2: Ches 4A 28
Sandon Rd. CH2: Ches 4K 27
Sandown Ct. CH5: Shot 4K 23
Sandown Rd. CH5: Shot 4J 23
Sandown Ter. CH3: Ches 7B 28
Sandpiper Ct. CH4: Ches 7H 37
Sandpiper Way CH4: Ches 6H 37
Sandringham Av. CH4: Ches 6C 28
Sandrock Rd. CH3: Chris 2G 39
Sandwood Av. CH4: Brou 6F 35
SANDYCROFT 5E 24
Sandycroft Ind. Est. CH5: Sand 5D 24
Sandy Gro. CH7: Mold 6E 30
Sandy La. CH3: Ches 7B 28
         CH3: Saig, Hunt 4D 38
         CH4: High K 5E 42
         CH4: Salt 3C 36
         CH5: Gard C 1D 24
         CH6: Bag 6K 5
         LL12: Hope .7A 42
Sandy Way CH5: Con Q 2E 22
         CH5: Haw 7J 23
Sark Ho. CH2: Ches 4D 28
Sarl Williams Ct. CH1: Ches 6J 27 (2B 44)
SAUGHALL 6A 16
Saughall Hey CH1: Saug 6A 16
Saughall Rd. CH1: Blac 3D 26
         CH1: Ches, Blac 3E 26
Saxon Way CH1: Blac 2D 26
Scholars Cl. CH4: Salt 3E 36
School La. CH2: Mick T 7G 19
         CH3: Guil S .3G 29
         CH6: Flint M 6G 11
         CH7: Coed 7B 40
         CH8: G'fld 1F 5
School St. CH2: Ches 5A 28
Scotch Row CH5: Man 6C 24
Scots Rd. CH5: Man 6B 24
Seahill Rd. CH1: Saug, Sea 2J 25
SEALAND 2J 25
Sealand Av. CH5: Gard C 1D 24
         CH8: Holy 5G 5
Sealand Ind. Est. CH1: Ches 6F 27
Sealand Rd. CH1: Sea, Ches 3A 26
         CH5: Sea 1E 24
Seathwaite Way CH5: Con Q 2E 22
Sea Vw. Ter. CH8: Holw 4C 4
Seaville St. CH1: Ches 6A 28
Sebring Av. CH7: Nor H 4D 22
Second Av. CH5: Dee I 4D 14
         CH6: Flint 2G 11
Sedgefield Rd. CH1: Ches 6H 27
Sedum Cl. CH3: Hunt 3C 38
Sefton Rd. CH2: Ches 4C 28
Selkirk Dr. CH4: Ches 2G 37
Selkirk Rd. CH4: Ches 2G 37
Seller St. CH1: Ches 6A 28 (3E 44)
Selsdon Cl. CH4: Buck 4C 32
Selsdon Ct. CH4: Ches 2J 37
Sens Cl. CH1: Ches 7J 27 (4A 44)
Serenity La. CH5: Dob 5K 33
Serpentine, The CH4: Ches 2H 37
Sevenacre Cl. CH6: Bag 4D 6

Sgwar y Capel CH5: Con Q 7G 13
                                            (off Chapel St.)
Shaftesbury Av. CH3: Ches 6D 28
Shaftesbury Dr. CH6: Flint 1E 10
Shakespeare Av. CH5: Ewl 2G 33
Shannon Cl. CH4: Salt 4E 36
Shavington Av. CH2: Ches 4B 28
Shaw Cl. CH5: Ewl .1G 33
Shed La. CH3: Ches 6D 28
Sheldon Av. CH3: Ches 6D 28
Shelley Cl. CH5: Ewl 1G 33
Shelley Rd. CH1: Blac 2E 26
Shepherd's La. CH2: Ches 3K 27
Sheraton Rd. CH3: Chris 4K 39
Sherbourne Av. CH4: Ches 4H 37
Sheridan Av. CH5: Ewl 1G 33
Sheringham Cl. CH4: Ches 4E 36
Sherwood Rd. CH1: Blac 3E 26
Shipbrook Rd. CH2: Upton 2B 28
Shipgate, The CH1: Ches 6C 44
Shipgate St. CH1: Ches 1K 37 (6C 44)
Shire Vw. CH7: Mold 4F 31
Shocklach Rd. CH2: Upton 2A 28
SHOTTON 2K 23
Shotton High Level Station (Rail) 2K 23
Shotton La. CH5: Ewl, Shot 6G 23
         CH5: Shot 3J 23
Shotton Station (Rail) 1K 23
SHOTWICK 3G 15
Shotwick Hall 2F 15
Shotwick-Helsby By-Pass
         CH1: Moll, Dunk, S'wck 3G 15
Shotwick Rd. CH5: Dee I 3C 14
Shotwick La. CH1: Wood 2G 15
Shrewsbury Way CH4: Salt 3F 37
Sibell St. CH1: Ches 6A 28 (2E 44)
Siddeley Cl. CH4: Brou 5G 35
Sidney Hall Ct. CH5: Con Q 3E 22
Signal Ct. CH2: Ches 6B 28
Silverbirch Cft. CH4: Brou 6F 35
Silverbirch Way CH4: Penf 2J 41
Silverdale Av. CH7: Drury 4H 33
Silverdale Pk. Ind. Est. CH2: Mick T 1H 29
Silvermuir CH1: Blac 5E 26
Silverstone Dr. CH7: Buck 5B 32
Simonstone Rd. CH4: Brou 5H 35
Simpson Cl. CH2: Mos 6J 17
Simpson Rd. CH2: Mos 6J 17
Simpsons Way CH4: Brou 6F 35
Sixth Av. CH5: Dee I 5C 14
         CH6: Flint 2G 11
Skips La. CH3: Chris 2G 39
Slack La. CH5: Haw 4J 33
                                            (not continuous)
Smiths Cotts. CH6: Bag 3K 5
                                            (off Bagillt Rd.)
Smithy Cl. CH1: Saug 6A 16
SMITHY GATE 6D 4
Smithy La. CH5: Ewl 7E 22
         CH7: Nor H .2B 22
Smithy Pathway CH4: Ches 5F 37
Snowdon Av. CH5: Con Q 1F 23
         CH7: Bryn B .3A 32
Snowdon Cres. CH4: Ches 4G 37
Somerford Rd. CH4: Brou 5G 35
Somerset Rd. CH2: Ches 3B 28
Somerset St. CH1: Ches 5K 27 (1C 44)
Sorrel Cl. CH3: Hunt 3C 38
Soughton Rd. CH7: All, New B 2K 31
SOUGHTON (SYCHDYN) 7G 21
Souters La. CH1: Ches 7K 27 (5D 44)
South Av. CH2: Ches 5A 28 (1E 44)
South Bank CH1: Ches 4J 27
         CH5: Shot 4K 23
South Cres. Rd. CH4: Ches 1A 38 (6E 44)
Southfields Cl. CH7: Buck 4C 32
South Grn. CH5: Sea 2E 24
South La. CH7: Buck 4C 32
South St. CH3: Ches 7C 28
South Vw. CH4: Ches 2K 37 (7D 44)
         CH7: Buck 6E 32
South Vw. Rd. CH1: Ches 6H 27 (3A 44)
South Way CH1: Blac 4E 26
Sovereign Way CH1: Ches 6E 26
Sparks Cl. CH3: Gt Bou 2D 38
Speedwell Cl. CH4: High K 4D 38
Spencer Ind. Est. CH7: Drury 3F 33
Spenser Cl. CH5: Ewl 1G 33
Spital Wlk. CH3: Ches 6B 28
SPON GREEN 6F 33
Spon Grn. CH7: Buck 6F 33
Springbank CH8: G'fld 3F 5
Springdale CH5: Haw 7J 23
Springfield CH5: Haw 1A 34
Springfield Cl. CH4: High K 2E 42
         CH5: Con Q .2E 22
         CH6: Flint 2F 11
Springfield Ct. CH4: High K 3E 42
Springfield Dr. CH2: Ches 4A 28
         CH7: Buck 5B 32
Springfield Hill CH8: Pen H 5J 9

Springfields CH2: Mick T 7G 19
         CH8: Holw 3D 4
Spring St. CH5: Con Q 1J 23
Springwood Cl. CH1: Blac 4C 26
Springy La. CH7: S'ton 5J 21
Square, The CH1: Ches 6A 28 (3E 44)
         CH3: Ches 1G 39
         CH7: M Isa 4K 31
Stadium Ind. Est., The CH1: Ches 5G 27
Stadium Way CH1: Ches 6G 27
Stafford Rd. CH5: Gard C 1D 24
Stainton Gro. CH5: Con Q 7E 12
Stamford Ct. CH3: Ches 6E 28
Stamford La. CH3: Cot E 5K 29
Stamford Rd. CH1: Blac 2E 26
Stamford Way CH5: Ewl 4D 22
         CH7: Nor H .4D 22
         CH8: Milwr 7G 5
Standard Rd. CH7: Drury 2F 33
Stanley Pk. Ct. CH4: Salt 4E 36
Stanley Pk. Dr. CH4: Salt 4E 36
Stanley Pl. CH1: Ches 7J 27 (4A 44)
         CH7: Mold 3J 23
Stanley Pl. M. CH1: Ches 5A 44
Stanley Rd. CH7: Buck 5C 32
Stanleys Est. CH7: Buck 5C 32
Stanley St. CH1: Ches 7J 27 (4A 44)
         CH7: Mold 5F 31
Stanney La. CH2: Back 3J 17
Stanton Dr. CH2: Ches 3K 27
Starkey La. CH7: Nor 1G 21
Station Cotts. CH1: Saug 1K 25
Station La. CH2: Mick T 7H 19
         CH3: Guil S .1H 29
         CH5: Haw 1A 34
Station Rd. CH1: Ches 5A 28 (1E 44)
         CH1: Lea B 5F 17
         CH5: Haw 1A 34
         CH5: Queen .3B 24
         CH6: Bag 3B 6
         CH7: Pade 2D 40
         CH8: G'fld 1H 5
         CH8: Holy 4F 5
Station Ter. CH5: Sand 5F 25
Station Vw. CH2: Ches 6B 28
Station Way CH4: Penf 2J 41
Steam Mill St. CH3: Ches 6A 28
Stearns Cl. CH1: Blac 3G 27
Steele St. CH1: Ches 7K 27 (5C 44)
Stendall Rd. CH1: Ches 5G 27
Stephen Gray Rd. CH7: Mold 6H 31
Steven Ct. CH3: Ches 6J 39
Stile End CH2: Mick T 7H 19
Stirling Cl. CH3: Ches 6C 28
STOAK 1C 18
Stocks Av. CH3: Ches 1C 38
Stocks La. CH3: Ches 7C 28
Stone Cft. CH3: Gt Bou 2D 38
Stoneleigh Cl. CH5: Gard C 2D 24
Stone Pl. CH2: Ches 5B 28
Stone Row CH5: Con Q 7G 13
                                            (off Church Hill)
STONEY HILL 5K 33
Strand CH8: Holy 5F 5
Strand Cl. CH8: Holy 4F 5
Strand Cres. CH8: Holy 4F 5
Strand La. CH8: Holy 4F 5
Strand Vw. CH8: G'fld 3F 5
                                            (off Greenfield Rd.)
Strand Wlk. CH8: Holy 5F 5
Stratford Rd. CH1: Blac 4E 26
Strawberry Flds. CH3: Gt Bou 2D 38
Strawberry La. CH1: Moll 2C 16
Street, The CH2: Mick T, Hoole V 1E 28
Strickland St. CH5: Shot 3K 23
Stringer's La. CH4: High K 5F 43
         LL12: Burt 5F 43
Stryd Henardd CH7: Mold 6F 31
Stryt Cae Rhedyn CH7: Lees 4A 40
Stryt Isa CH4: Hope, Penf 4G 41
         LL12: Hope 7J 41
Stuart Cl. CH3: Ches 5E 28
Stuart Pl. CH1: Ches 6K 27 (2D 44)
Stubbs Pl. CH1: Blac 5E 26
Suffolk Ho. CH1: Ches 3E 44
Summerdale Rd. CH5: Aston 4J 23
Summerfield Cl. CH4: Brou 6E 34
Summerfield Rd. CH3: Guil S 3H 29
Summerville Cl. CH5: Con Q 1F 23
Sumner Rd. CH1: Blac 4E 26
Sumpter Pathway CH7: Ches 5B 28
Sunbury Cres. CH4: Ches 3F 37
Sundawn Av. CH8: Holy 5G 5
Suningdale CH7: Buck 3C 32
Sunny Ridge CH7: Mold 3E 30
Sunnyside CH5: Man 6B 24
Sunnyside Cl. CH6: Bag 4K 5
Surrey Rd. CH2: Ches 3C 28
Sussex Rd. CH2: Ches 4B 28
Sussex Way CH2: Ches 3B 28

Sutherland Way CH3: Ches 5D 28
Sutton Cl. CH2: Mick T 7H 19
CH5: Con Q 3E 22
Sutton Dr. CH2: Ches 3A 28
Swain Av. CH7: Buck 6F 33
Swan La. CH7: G'nydd 7B 30
Swan St. CH6: Flint .7G 7
Swan Wlk. CH6: Flint 1G 11
(off Duke St.)
Swinchiard La. CH6: Flint 1G 11
Swinchiard Wlk. CH6: Flint 1G 11
Swinleys Hey CH3: Gt Bou 2C 38
Swn y Gwynt CH6: Flint 3H 11
Swn-y-Nant CH7: Mold 6F 31
Sycamore Av. CH5: Con Q 1G 23
Sycamore Cl. CH5: Haw 2H 33
Sycamore Dr. CH4: Ches 4E 36
CH7: Lees 5B 40
Sycamore Gro. CH4: Brou 6F 35
Sycamore Ter. CH8: G'fld 1G 5
(off Englefield Rd.)
Sychdyn Rd. CH7: Nor 6G 21
Sydney Rd. CH1: Ches 5H 27
Sydney St. CH6: Flint 1G 11
Sydney Wlk. CH6: Flint 1G 11
Sylvan M. CH1: Blac 2E 26

T

Tabernacle St. CH7: Buck 5D 32
Talbot St. CH1: Ches 5K 27 (1D 44)
Talbot Ter. CH6: Bag .4C 6
Talfryn Cl. CH5: Con Q 6F 13
Talgarreg Dr. CH5: Con Q 4E 22
Taliesin Av. CH5: Shot 2J 23
Tan y Bryn CH7: Buck 3C 32
Tan-y-Bryn CH7: S'ton 7G 21
CH8: G'fld .1G 5
Tan y Coed CH7: S'ton 1G 31
Tan-y-Coed CH7: Mold 5E 30
CH8: Carm .3B 4
Tan-y-Felin CH8: G'fld 2F 5
Tan-y-Graig CH7: Mold 5D 30
Tan-yr-Ysgol CH7: S'ton 7G 21
Tarrant Cl. CH1: Moll 6F 17
Tarvin Rd. CH3: Ches 7C 28
CH3: L'ton, Chris 6F 29
Tatton Cl. CH4: Ches 4E 36
Taylors Vw. CH5: Shot 3J 23
Taynton Cl. CH5: Con Q 1E 22
Tecwyn Dr. CH5: Con Q 7E 12
Tegid Way CH4: Salt 4D 36
Telford Ct. CH1: Dunk 1D 16
Telford Way CH4: Salt 3F 37
Temple Chambers CH1: Ches 3C 44
Tennyson Ct. CH5: Ewl 1H 33
Tennyson Wlk. CH1: Blac 3G 27
Tenth Av. CH5: Dee I 4B 14
(not continuous)
Terrace La. CH4: Penf 2K 41
Terrig Cres. CH7: Buck 5D 32
Terrig St. CH5: Shot 4K 23
Tewkesbury Cl. CH2: Upton 1B 28
Thackeray Dr. CH3: Ches 5E 28
Thackeray Towers CH1: Ches 2E 44
Third Av. CH5: Dee I 6D 14
CH6: Flint .2G 11
Thirlmere Rd. CH2: Ches 3C 28
Thomas Av. CH5: Ewl 1G 33
Thomas Brassey Cl. CH2: Ches 5A 28
Thomas Cl. CH1: Blac 2F 27
CH2: Mick T 7H 19
Thomas Row CH6: Bag 2B 6
(off High St.)
Thomas St. CH6: Flint 7H 7
Thornberry Cl. CH1: Saug 7B 16
Thornfield Av. CH5: Con Q 2H 23
Thornfields CH5: Shot 4J 23
Thornhill Cl. CH4: Brou 6D 34
Thornton Dr. CH2: Ches 3K 27
Three Old Arches CH1: Ches 5C 44
Threos Cl. CH5: Con Q 4E 22
Thursfield Ct. CH1: Ches 7H 27
(off New Crane St.)
Thurston Rd. CH4: Salt 4E 36
Tilers Cl. CH7: Buck 4C 32
Timberfields Rd. CH1: Saug 7A 16
Tintern Av. CH2: Upton 2B 28
Tir Wat CH7: M Isa 5A 32
Tir y Ffrith La. CH7: Ponty 7B 40
Titian Cl. CH5: Con Q 7E 12
Tivaton Cl. CH5: Con Q 2F 23
Tiverton Cl. CH2: Ches 3A 28
Toft Cl. CH4: Ches 4E 36
Toll Bar Rd. CH3: Gt Bou 7E 28
Tollemache Ter. CH2: Ches 6B 28
Tomkinson St. CH2: Ches 5A 28
Tomlins Ter. CH1: Blac 3E 26
(off Burton Rd.)
Toogood Cl. CH2: Mick T 7H 19

Top Works CH6: Bag .2A 6
Totland Gro. CH2: Ches 4A 28
Tourist Info. Cen.
Chester 7K 27 (5D 44)
Ewloe 6D 22
Mold 5F 31
Tower Gdns. CH8: Holy 5F 5
Towergate CH1: Ches 4A 44
Tower Rd. CH1: Ches 6H 27 (3A 44)
Towers Way CH4: Penf 2H 41
Tower Wharf CH1: Ches 6J 27 (3A 44)
Townfield La. CH1: Moll 3D 16
Toy Mus. 7K 27 (5C 44)
Trafford St. CH1: Ches 5K 27 (1C 44)
Tram La. CH7: Buck .4E 32
Tram Rd. CH7: Buck 3E 32
Tramway St. CH1: Ches 6A 28 (2E 44)
Trebor Av. CH6: Bag .5C 6
Treborth Rd. CH1: Blac 5D 26
Trefoil Cl. CH3: Hunt 3D 38
Tregele Cl. CH1: Blac 5D 26
Trelawney Sq. CH6: Flint 7G 7
Trelawny Av. CH6: Flint 1H 11
Trelech Ct. CH5: Con Q 4E 22
Trem Afon CH7: M Isa 4K 31
Trem y Foel CH7: S'ton 1G 31
Trinity Rd. CH8: G'fld .2G 5
Trinity St. CH1: Ches 7J 27 (4B 44)
Tros-yr-Aber CH8: G'fld 2F 5
Tros y Waen CH6: Flint M 6G 11
Trueman's Ct. CH5: Haw 1A 34
Trueman's Way CH5: Haw 1A 34
Trym yr Hydref CH7: Nor H 4C 22
Tudor Av. CH6: Flint .3G 11
Tudor Cl. CH5: Shot .3K 23
CH7: Nor H 4B 22
CH8: Holy .5E 4
Tudor Grn. CH1: Blac 2E 26
Tudor Way CH3: Gt Bou 2C 38
Tuscan Way CH5: Con Q 7G 13
Tushingham Cl. CH3: Gt Bou 2D 38
Twain Cl. CH5: Ewl .1G 33
Tyddyn Messham CH6: Bag 5D 6
Tyddyn St. CH7: Mold 5F 31
Tyn Twll La. CH6: Bag 6J 5

U

UGC Cinema
Chester 5F 27
Ullswater Cres. CH2: Ches 2C 28
Ullswater Rd. CH7: Buck 3F 33
Union Ct. CH1: Ches 6A 28
(off Canalside)
Union Pl. CH1: Ches 5B 44
Union St. CH1: Ches 7A 28 (4E 44)
Union Ter. CH1: Ches 6K 27 (3D 44)
Union Wlk. CH1: Ches 7K 27 (4D 44)
Unity Pas. CH1: Ches 7K 27 (5C 44)
University College Chester 5H 27 (1A 44)
Uplands Av. CH5: Con Q 3F 23
Up. Aston Hall La. CH5: Haw 7K 23
Up. Bryn Coch CH7: Mold 7D 30
Up. Bryn Coch La. CH7: Mold 6D 30
Up. Bryn Rd. CH5: Con Q 7F 13
Up. Cambrian Rd. CH1: Ches 6H 27 (2A 44)
Up. Northgate St. CH1: Ches 6J 27 (2B 44)
(not continuous)
Up. River Bank CH6: Bag 3J 5
UPTON 1A 28
Upton Dr. CH2: Upton 2J 27
UPTON HEATH 7A 18
Upton La. CH2: Upton 1J 27
Upton Pk. CH2: Upton 2K 27
Uwch-y-Dre CH7: G'nydd 7B 30
Uwch-y-Mor CH8: Pen H 5H 9
Uwch-y-Nant CH7: M Isa 4K 31

V

Vale Av. CH5: Haw 2G 33
Vale Cl. CH4: Brou 6G 35
Vale Dr. CH7: M Isa .5K 31
Valley Dr. CH2: Ches 3J 27
Vaughans La. CH3: Gt Bou 1C 38
Vaughan Way CH5: Con Q 3F 23
Venables Rd. CH1: Ches 4F 27
Vermeer Cl. CH5: Con Q 7E 12
Vernay Grn. CH4: Ches 4H 37
Vernon Cl. CH1: Saug 7A 16
Vernon Rd. CH1: Ches 6H 27
Vetches, The CH3: Guil S 3H 29
Vicarage Cl. CH3: Guil S 3H 29
Vicarage Rd. CH2: Ches 5B 28
CH6: Bag 4C 6
VICARSCROSS 5G 29
Vicars Cross Ct. CH3: Ches 6D 28
Vicars Cross Rd. CH3: Ches 6D 28

Vicar's La. CH1: Ches 7K 27 (5D 44)
Vickers Cl. CH5: Haw 5A 24
Victoria Av. CH7: Buck 4E 32
Victoria Ct. CH2: Ches 5J 27 (1B 44)
Victoria Cres. CH2: Ches 5J 27 (1B 44)
CH4: Ches 1A 38 (6E 44)
CH5: Shot 2J 23
CH7: Ponty 7C 40
Victoria Pk. CH6: Bag 4J 5
Victoria Pathway CH4: Ches 1A 38 (7E 44)
Victoria Pl. CH1: Ches 6K 27 (3D 44)
Victoria Rd. CH2: Ches 5J 27 (1B 44)
CH4: Salt .3D 36
CH5: Shot 2J 23
CH6: Bag .4K 5
CH7: Buck 4E 32
CH7: Mold 5F 31
Victoria Ter. CH7: Mold 4G 31
Victory Ct. CH7: Mold 6G 31
Viking Way CH5: Con Q 7E 12
Village Rd. CH3: Chris 1G 39
CH3: Wav .5K 39
CH7: Nor, Nor H 3J 21
Villa Rd. CH5: Sea 1F 25
Vincent Dr. CH4: Ches 3H 37
Virginia Dr. CH1: Blac 3C 26
Volunteer St. CH1: Ches 7K 27 (5C 44)
Vounog Hill CH4: Penf 3J 41
Vownog CH7: Buck 6G 21
Vownog, The CH7: S'ton 6H 21
Vownog Newydd CH7: S'ton 6H 21
Vyrnwy Rd. CH4: Salt 3D 36

W

WAEN-ISAF 6H 11
WAEN-TROCHWAED 7D 8
WAEN-Y-BALLS 6G 11
Walker St. CH2: Ches 5A 28
Walls Av. CH1: Ches 7H 27 (4A 44)
Walmoor Hill CH3: Ches 1C 38
Walmoor Pk. CH3: Ches 7C 28
Walnut Cl. CH2: Upton 1K 27
Walpole Av. CH5: Haw 1J 33
Walpole St. CH1: Ches 5J 27 (1A 44)
Walter St. CH1: Ches 5K 27 (1C 44)
Waltham Pl. CH4: Ches 3G 37
Walton Pl. CH1: Blac 4E 26
Waltons, The CH4: Ches 3A 38
WAL-WEN 3K 5
WALWEN 7C 8
Walwen Isaf CH6: Bag 3K 5
Walwen Uchaf CH6: Bag 4K 5
Wards Ter. CH2: Ches 5B 28
Wared Dr. CH7: Nor H 4B 22
Warren Cres. CH7: Buck 5H 33
Warren Dr. CH4: Brou 6E 34
Warren Hall Ct. CH4: Brou 7C 34
Warrington Rd. CH2: Hoole V, Ches, Mick T . . .3D 28
Warwick Rd. CH1: Blac 3F 27
Washington Dr. CH5: Ewl 6J 23
Watergate Row Nth. CH1: Ches 7J 27 (4B 44)
Watergate Row Sth. CH1: Ches 7J 27 (5B 44)
Watergate Sq. CH1: Ches 7J 27 (5A 44)
Watergate St. CH1: Ches 7J 27 (5A 44)
Waterloo Rd. CH2: Ches 4J 27
Waters Edge CH1: Ches 6H 27 (3A 44)
WATERS GREEN 7K 33
(off Hoole La.)
Waterside Cl. CH3: Ches 6B 28
Waterside Vw. CH1: Ches 6K 27 (3C 44)
Waters Reams CH3: Gt Bou 1D 38
Water St. CH7: Mold .5F 31
Water Tower 6J 27 (3A 44)
Water Twr. St. CH1: Ches 6J 27 (3B 44)
Watertower Vw. CH2: Ches 6B 28
Waterway CH3: Wav .4K 39
Watery La. CH7: Buck 6B 32
Watkin St. CH5: Sand 5E 24
Watling Ct. CH3: Ches 6E 28
Watling Cres. CH4: Ches 2K 37
Wats Dyke Av. CH8: Holy 4F 5
CH7: M Isa 4K 31
Wat's Dyke Way CH7: S'ton 6H 21
Watson's Cl. CH4: Brou 6G 35
Wat's Rd. CH4: Penf .3J 41
Watts Cl. CH7: Buck .5B 32
Wavells Way CH3: Hunt 4D 38
Waverley Ter. CH7: Buck 4A 28
WAVERTON 4J 39
Waverton Bus. Pk. CH3: Wav 5H 39
Waverton Mill Quays CH3: Wav 4K 39
Waverton Pk. CH3: Wav 4K 39
(off Guy La.)
Wavertree Rd. CH1: Blac 3C 26
Wayside Ct. CH2: Mick T 7H 19
Wealstone Ct. CH2: Ches 3A 28
Wealstone La. CH2: Upton 2K 27
Weaver Gro. CH2: Mick T 7H 19
Weaver St. CH1: Ches 7J 27 (5B 44)

Webster Cl. CH4: Brou 6G 35
Wedgewood Hgts. CH8: Holy 4D 4
Wedgewood Rd. CH5: Aston 5K 23
Weighbridge Rd. CH5: Dee I 3H 13
Welland Dr. CH5: Con Q 1F 23
Wellfield Vw. CH7: Nor H 4B 22
Well Ho. Dr. CH4: Penym 1K 41
Wellington Cl. CH5: Haw 1H 33
Wellington Pl. CH1: Ches 2D 44
Wellington Rd. CH4: Brou 6F 35
Wellington St. CH5: Shot 2K 23
Well La. CH1: Moll .6F 17
   CH2: Ches 3A 28
Wells Cl. CH2: Mick T 7H 19
Well St. CH7: Buck, M Isa 6B 32
   CH8: Holy 4F 5
                 (Greenfield St.)
   CH8: Holy *5F 5*
                (off Whitford St.)
Welsh Rd. CH1: Wood, S'wck 3G 15
   CH4: Bald, D'ton 1K 43
   CH5: Gard C 2C 24
   CH5: Sea 7E 14
Wemyss Rd. CH1: Blac 4D 26
Wenlock Cres. CH5: Man 5C 24
Wenlock Way CH4: Salt 3F 37
Wentworth Cl. CH7: Buck 3C 32
WEPRE 2J 23
Wepre Country Pk. .3G 23
Wepre Country Pk. Vis. Cen. 3G 23
Wepre Ct. CH5: Con Q 3F 23
Wepre Dr. CH5: Con Q 2J 23
Wepre Hall Cres. CH5: Con Q 2G 23
Wepre La. CH5: Con Q 4F 23
   CH7: Nor H 4D 22
Wepre Pk. CH5: Con Q 2G 23
Wern Av. CH6: Bag .4C 6
Wern Ucha CH6: Bag 4B 6
WERVIN 3C 18
Wervin Mobile Home Pk. CH2: Wer 3C 18
Wervin Rd. CH2: Stoak, C'ton 2B 18
   CH2: Wer, Upton 2C 18
Wesley Pl. CH7: Mold 3F 31
Wesley St. CH5: Con Q 1H 23
West Bank CH1: Ches 4J 27
Westbourne Cres. CH7: Buck 5C 32
Westbourne Rd. CH1: Ches 4G 27
Westbrook Dr. CH7: Buck 6E 32
Westbury Dr. CH7: Buck 5G 33
Westbury Way CH4: Ches 3F 37
West Dr. CH8: Holy .5E 4
Western App. CH2: Ches 4A 28
Western Av. CH1: Blac 5C 26
Western Av. Shop. Mall *CH1: Blac* *4D 26*
               (off Western Av.)
Western Ct. CH5: Ches 4A 28
Westfield Cl. CH4: Ches 2H 37
Westfield Dr. CH4: Penf 3H 41
Westgate Street Gallery 4B 44
West Grn. CH5: Sea .2E 24
W. Lorne St. CH1: Ches 6J 27 (2A 44)
Westminster Av. CH4: Ches 3H 37
Westminster Ct. *CH2: Ches* *6B 28*
               (off Lightfoot St.)
Westminster Cres. CH5: Shot 3A 24
Westminster Grn. CH4: Ches 2K 37 (7C 44)
Westminster Rd. CH2: Ches 5B 28
   CH4: Brou 6F 35
Westminster Ter. CH4: Ches 2J 37 (7B 44)
Weston Cl. CH5: Gard C 2D 24
Weston Gro. CH2: Upton 2A 28
W. Shotwick La. CH1: S'wck 3F 15
West St. CH2: Ches 5A 28 (1E 44)
West Vw. CH4: Penf 4J 41
   CH7: Buck 6E 32
   CH7: Mold 5F 31
West Vw. Dr. CH7: M Isa 5J 31
Westward Rd. CH3: Ches 1C 38
Westway CH5: Man .6C 24
Wetherby Cl. CH1: Ches 6H 27
Weybourne Cl. CH4: Ches 4E 36
Whaddon Dr. CH4: Ches 5F 37
Wharf, The *CH1: Ches* *6H 27*
              (off New Crane St.)

Wharfdale Av. CH5: Con Q 2F 23
Wheldon Cl. CH2: Upton 7A 18
WHELSTON 4J 5
Whipcord La. CH1: Ches 5H 27 (3A 44)
Whitby Av. CH2: Ches 3K 27
Whitby Rd. CH1: Back 1G 17
Whitchurch Rd. CH3: Gt Bou, Chris 7D 28
   CH3: Row, Hat H, Wav 3H 39
Whitcross Cl. CH5: Con Q 1E 22
White Farm Rd. CH7: All 2C 32
White Friars CH1: Ches 7J 27 (5B 44)
White La. CH3: Chris 2F 39
White Oaks Dr. CH7: Nor H 4C 22
White Rock Rd. CH4: Penym 1K 41
Whites Mdw. CH3: Gt Bou 2C 38
White Way Gro. CH5: Gard C 2D 24
Whitford Rd. CH8: Whit 2A 4
Whitford St. CH8: Holy 4E 4
Whittle Cl. CH5: Sand 5E 24
Whitton Dr. CH2: Upton 3A 28
Wicker La. CH3: Guil S 3H 29
Wiend, The CH2: Ches 4K 27
Wigdale, The CH5: Haw 1A 34
Wilde Cl. CH5: Ewl .1G 33
Wildmoor La. CH3: Lit B 6K 19
Willan Rd. CH1: Blac 4D 26
Williams Cl. CH2: Ches 4J 27
   CH4: Penym 1K 41
William St. CH1: Ches 6K 27 (3C 44)
   CH2: Ches 5B 28
Willow, The CH7: Buck 2D 32
Willoway Rd. CH3: Ches 6D 28
Willow Cl. CH2: Upton 7K 17
   CH7: Buck 5G 33
Willow Ct. CH4: High K 3E 42
   CH5: Con Q *6F 13*
               (off King's Rd.)
Willow Cres. CH2: Ches 4C 28
   CH5: Con Q 1F 23
   CH5: Haw 1H 33
Willow Dr. CH1: Blac 3D 26
   CH6: Flint 2E 10
Willowfield Est. CH8: Pen H 4H 9
Willow Gro. CH2: Ches 4D 28
   CH7: Buck 2C 32
Willowherb Cl. CH3: Hunt 3C 38
Willow Ho. CH1: Ches 6E 26
Willow La. CH5: Pen 4C 24
Willow Lea CH1: Moll 5F 17
Willow Pk. CH5: Queen 6A 24
Willow Rd. CH4: Ches 3F 37
   CH7: Lees 5B 30
Willow Wlk. CH7: Lees 4A 30
Willow Way CH4: Brou 6F 35
Wilton Rd. CH5: Man 6B 24
WIMBOLDS TRAFFORD 2H 19
Winchester Sq. CH4: Ches 4F 37
Windermere Av. CH2: Ches 2C 28
   CH5: Con Q 1H 23
WINDMILL 6H 9
Windmill Cl. CH7: Buck 4D 32
   CH8: Holy 5G 5
Windmill La. CH3: Chris 1G 39
Windmill Ri. CH2: Upton 1K 27
Windmill Rd. CH7: Buck 4D 32
Windmill Ter. CH8: Pen H 6J 9
Windsor Av. CH5: Con Q 2H 23
   CH5: Shot 2K 23
Windsor Ct. CH1: Ches 1K 37 (6D 44)
Windsor Dr. CH4: Brou 6E 34
   CH6: Flint 1E 10
Windsor Pk. CH8: Carm 3B 4
Windsor Rd. CH4: Ches 3F 37
Winkwell Dr. CH4: Ches 4J 27
Winscombe Dr. CH3: Ches 6E 28
Winsford Way CH1: Ches 5B 26
Winston Ct. CH2: Ches 3C 28
Wirral Vw. CH5: Con Q 1F 23
   CH5: Haw 7J 23
Withy Cft. CH3: Gt Bou 2D 38
Woburn Dr. CH2: Upton 1B 28
Wold Cft. CH5: Haw 1A 34
Wood, The CH4: Penym 7K 33
   CH5: Dob 7K 33
Wood Av. CH4: Brou 6F 35

WOODBANK 1J 15
Woodbank La. CH1: Wood 3G 15
Woodbank Rd. CH5: Con Q 2G 23
Wood Cft. CH3: Guil S 4H 29
Woodcroft CH7: Drury 3G 33
Woodfield Av. CH6: Flint 2H 11
Woodfield Cl. CH4: Brou 6E 34
   CH5: Con Q 2G 23
Woodfield Gro. CH2: Ches 3D 28
Woodfield Ho. CH2: Ches 3C 28
Woodfields CH3: Chris 2G 39
Wood Grn. CH7: Mold 5G 31
Wood Gro. CH7: Lees 5B 40
Woodhall Av. CH4: Salt 3E 36
Woodland Bank CH2: Mick T 6H 19
Woodland Ct. CH5: Man 7C 24
   CH6: Flint 2F 11
Woodland Cres. CH5: Shot 2J 23
Woodland Dr. CH6: Flint 2F 11
   CH8: G'fld 2F 5
Woodlands CH7: Mold 5G 31
Woodlands, The CH5: Dob 5J 33
Woodlands Av. CH1: Ches 4H 27
Woodlands Cl. CH7: Mold 5G 31
Woodlands Ct. CH5: Haw 1A 34
Woodlands Dr. CH2: Ches 4A 28
   CH5: Haw 2H 33
Woodlands La. CH3: Ches 6C 28
Woodlands Rd. CH3: Hunt 3C 38
   CH4: Ches 2G 37
   CH7: Mold 5G 31
Woodland St. CH5: Shot 2J 23
Wood La. CH4: Brou 5F 35
   CH4: Penf 2J 41
   CH5: Haw 2G 33
   CH8: Holy 4G 5
Woodlea Av. CH2: Upton 1B 28
Woodside Cl. CH5: Ewl 7J 23
Woodside Ct. CH1: Ches 4J 27
Woodside Rd. CH1: Blac 3C 26
Wood St. CH5: Sand 5E 24
Wood Ville CH5: Man 6B 24
Woodville Gdns. CH7: S'ton 7F 21
Worcester Pl. CH1: Blac 4G 27
Wordsworth Cl. CH5: Ewl 1G 33
Wordsworth Cres. CH1: Blac 3F 27
Wordsworth M. CH1: Blac 3G 27
Wordsworth Sq. CH1: Blac 3F 27
Worsley Av. CH1: Saug 7A 16
Worthington Ct. CH2: Ches 4K 27
Wrekin Way CH4: Ches 3F 37
Wrexham Rd. CH4: Ches, Ecc, Marl L 7F 37
   CH4: Penf 4J 41
   CH7: Mold 6F 31
   LL12: Hope 5J 41
Wrexham St. CH7: Mold 5F 31
Wroxham Cl. CH2: Ches 5K 27 (1C 44)
Wycliffe Ct. CH2: Ches 6C 28
Wylfa Av. CH7: M Isa 4J 31
Wyndham Rd. CH1: Blac 4C 26
Wynnstay Rd. CH4: Brou 5G 35

Y

Yarrow Cl. CH4: Brou 6G 35
Y Caldias CH5: Con Q 4E 22
Y Dolydd CH7: Mold 6E 30
Yerburgh St. CH2: Ches 4K 27
Yew Tree Cl. CH4: Brou 6G 35
Y Fedwen Arian CH4: Penym 7J 33
Y Gilfach CH7: Mold 6F 31
Yonne, The CH1: Ches 7J 27 (4A 44)
York Av. CH5: Shot .3K 23
York Dr. CH2: Mick T 6G 19
York Rd. CH5: Con Q 6E 12
York St. CH1: Ches 6K 27 (3D 44)
Yowley Rd. CH5: Ewl 6H 23
Yr Ydlan CH7: M Isa 3K 31
Ystad Goffa Ct. *CH6: Flint* *2H 11*
                (off Maes Alaw)
Y Waen CH6: Flint M 6G 11